PROBLEM GAMBLING AND ITS TREATMENT

ABOUT THE AUTHOR

Ronald M. Pavalko, received his doctorate in sociology in 1963 from the University of California at Los Angeles. He has been a faculty member and administrator at the University of Wisconsin-Madison, Florida State University, and the University of Wisconsin-Parkside, Kenosha, Wisconsin, where he is currently Emeritus Professor of Sociology.

His publications in the field of gambling studies include *Risky Business: America's Fascination with Gambling*, Wadsworth, 2000; "A Case Study of a Casino Campaign: Testing the Dombrink-Thompson Model," in the fall 1999 issue of the *Journal of Gambling Studies*; "Problem Gambling: The Hidden Addiction," in the fall 1999 issue of *National Forum: The Phi Kappa Phi Journal*; and Problem Gambling Among Older People," in Anne M. Gurnack, Roland Atkinson, and Nancy Osgood, (eds.) *Treating Alcohol and Drug Use in the Elderly*, New York: Springer Publishing Company, (2001).

He is a member of the National Council on Problem Gambling, the Florida Council on Compulsive Gambling, and the Wisconsin Council on Problem Gambling.

PROBLEM GAMBLING AND ITS TREATMENT

An Introduction

By

RONALD M. PAVALKO, Ph.D.

Emeritus Professor of Sociology
University of Wisconsin - Parkside
Kenosha, Wisconsin

Charles C Thomas
PUBLISHER • LTD.
SPRINGFIELD • ILLINOIS • U.S.A.

Published and Distributed Throughout the World by

CHARLES C THOMAS • PUBLISHER, LTD.
2600 South First Street
Springfield, Illinois 62704

©2001 by CHARLES C THOMAS • PUBLISHER, LTD.

ISBN 0-398-07229-9 (hard)
ISBN 0-398-07230-2 (paper)

Library of Congress Catalog Card Number: 2001034727

With THOMAS BOOKS *careful attention is given to all details of man-
ufacturing and design. It is the Publisher's desire to present books that are satisfactory as to their physical qualities and artistic possibilities and appropriate for their particular use.* THOMAS BOOKS *will be true to those laws
of quality that assure a good name and good will.*

Printed in the United States of America
CR-R-3

Library of Congress Cataloging-in-Publication Data

Pavalko, Ronald M.
    Problem gambling and its treatment : an introduction / by
Ronald M. Pavalko.
        p. cm.
    Includes bibliographical references and index.
    ISBN 0-398-07229-9 (hard) -- ISBN 0-398-07230-2 (pbk.)
    1. Compulsive gambling. 2. Compulsive gambling--Treatment.
I. Title.

RC569.5.G35 P385 2001
616.85616.85'841--dc21

                                                2001034727

This book is dedicated to my grandchildren:
Whitney, Parker, and Porter

PREFACE

Legalized gambling has expanded dramatically in the United States and other countries since the 1960s. Along with this expansion, clinicians, counselors, researchers, and public policy makers have come to realize that as opportunities to gamble increase, increasing numbers of people gamble, and they gamble more frequently; as more people gamble, more people get into financial and other difficulties related to their gambling. They become "problem gamblers," addicted to gambling as surely as other people become addicted to alcohol or other drugs.

This book is an introduction to the topic of problem gambling and its treatment. The decision to write it reflects the author's personal commitment to promoting a better understanding of problem gambling and the belief that a need for a comprehensive overview of this topic exists in several quarters. I hope that one audience for this book will be college students taking courses in counseling, mental health and illness, social work, social problems, and public policy; and, more generally, students interested in pursuing careers in counseling and human/social service agencies. Public policymakers involved in the legalization, expansion, and regulation of commercial gambling are another audience that, I believe, needs an understanding of gambling's "downside," i.e., problem gambling. I have also tried to write this book using no more technical social/behavioral science "jargon" than absolutely necessary, with the hope that lay readers will find it interesting and valuable. Finally, I hope that, among those lay readers, problem gamblers and the relatives and friends of problem gamblers may gain some insight into how problem gambling manifests itself and what can be done about it.

A NOTE ON METHODOLOGY:
HOW DO WE KNOW WHAT WE KNOW?

Throughout this book, a variety of different data and information will be drawn upon to understand problem gambling and its treatment. What we know about problem gambling comes from different sources, which vary in their reliability, validity, and how well we can generalize from them. Another way of putting this is that "not all data are created equal."

One of the main things I will try to do is use data based on solid research whenever possible. This includes the results of both survey research and case studies. When using such research, we need to ask questions such as: how representative is the sample or study population of the universe we are trying to understand; were the questions asked of respondents clear and unambiguous; if the research was done in a particular part of the country, can the findings be generalized to the country as a whole? In effect, we always need to ask about the methodological soundness of the research we are using. A good example of the caution needed comes from research done on a core issue like the basic social and psychological characteristics of problem gamblers. A good deal of what we know about problem gamblers comes from studies of members of Gamblers Anonymous. If we try to generalize from such studies to "problem gamblers," we run into difficulties. Clearly, members of Gamblers Anonymous are not representative of all problem gamblers. After all, they have sought help from a self-help program, whereas most problem gamblers have not. "Gamblers Anonymous members" are very different from "problem gamblers."

There are ways of obtaining knowledge about problem gambling other than through systematic research. The relative newness of "gambling studies" (and problem gambling in particular) as a subject of research means that there are many issues on which we do not have solid research. It is essential to rely on other sources of information.

Counselors who treat problem gamblers and their families have a wealth of information about the gambling addiction process, the impact of problem gambling on families, barriers to treatment, what triggers relapse, etc. This is knowledge based on professional experience that comes from repeated encounters with problem gamblers.

When counselors describe problem gamblers and the treatment process, there is always the nagging question of just how representative a given counselor's clients are of problem gamblers in treatment, let alone all problem gamblers. Are they typical, or are they unique in some way? Because counselors are focused on treatment and concerned with bringing about changes in the behavior of their clients, they rarely ask such questions. But these are questions that must be asked when we try to incorporate the experience-based knowledge of counselors into our understanding of problem gambling. When consensus exists among counselors, we can be more confident about the validity of their observations. This is especially true if a number of counselors treating clients with different social and demographic characteristics (e.g., age, gender, ethnicity, region of the country) report seeing the same or similar phenomena. As an example of this, many if not most counselors report that clients who develop problems playing video poker machines do so very rapidly. Among counselors, video poker machines are commonly referred to as "the crack cocaine of gambling" (making an analogy with how quickly people become addicted to crack cocaine). This generalization has become the "conventional wisdom" among counselors, even though there is no "research" to support it. It remains a hypothesis to be empirically tested. That does not mean that it is not useful information. It can be used to understand the gambling problems of some people. We simply need to be careful not to treat this experience-based observation the same as factual knowledge established by rigorous, empirical research.

Another source of information about gambling can be useful. This consists of the individual experiences of recreational gamblers, problem gamblers, and recovering problem gamblers, all of whom have "stories to tell." They all have had experiences, good and bad, with gambling. They have personal "insights" into gambling, problem gambling, what works and doesn't work in recovery, etc. The difficulty in using those experiences and insights to come to a general understanding of gambling should be fairly obvious. It is very difficult to separate the unique experiences from the more general ones. As with the knowledge of counselors, when we hear the same experiences being recounted by different people, the information contained in them becomes more credible. They, too, can be a valuable source of hypotheses to be tested.

Finally, there are more and less informed "opinions" about gambling and problem gambling that are not based in any of the foregoing sources of knowledge. Gambling is a topic on which many people have many opinions. We need to be extremely careful to not convert opinions into information based on experience with gambling, let alone facts based on sound research.

ORGANIZATION OF THIS BOOK

This book follows what I believe is a logical sequence, starting with the development of an understanding of problem gambling and ending with a discussion of different kinds of treatment.

Chapter 1 deals with various terms that have been used to describe problem gambling. Because the study of problem gambling has borrowed many ideas and concepts from the field of chemical addiction, this chapter also examines the concepts of use, abuse, dependence, and addiction as they apply to problem gambling. Also discussed is the "medical model" of deviant behavior and its relevance to problem gambling.

The focus of Chapter 2 is problem gambling as an addiction. Similarities with and differences from chemical addiction are dealt with, as well as the behavior that distinguishes problem gamblers from recreational gamblers. An important goal of this chapter is developing an understanding of how gambling addiction progresses over time. The distinction between escape and action gamblers, securities trading as a form of gambling, and internet gambling is also discussed.

Chapter 3 focuses on the assessment and diagnosis of problem gambling. The development and use of several diagnostic instruments is discussed, and case studies are included to illustrate the diagnostic process.

How widespread, or prevalent, is problem gambling? Chapter 4 deals with this question. State and national studies are summarized, as well as research from other societies. This chapter also examines problem gambling prevalence rates in terms of standard demographic variables (gender, race/ethnicity, education, income, marital status), with special emphasis on age (gambling and problem gambling among youth and the elderly).

The social costs of problem gambling are the subject of Chapter 5. Included here are financial and psychological costs to families, financial institutions, the criminal justice system, the human service system, and employers. Both quantitative and qualitative data are used to illustrate these social costs.

How people find their way to treatment and obstacles to seeking treatment are dealt with in Chapter 6. Denial of a problem and embarrassment about admitting to a gambling problem serve as serious deterrents to seeking treatment.

In Chapter 7 the primary strategies for treating problem gambling, behavioral and cognitive therapy, are discussed. Relapse (returning to gambling after a period of recovery) is dealt with too. This chapter also presents a discussion of the treatment of the families of problem gamblers, as well as a review of research on the effectiveness of treatment programs.

Gamblers Anonymous, a self-help recovery group, is discussed in Chapter 8. Although modeled after the better known Alcoholics Anonymous, many significant differences exist between the two programs. In addition to pointing out these differences, this chapter identifies how Gamblers Anonymous attempts to change the behavior and thinking of problem gamblers. It concludes with a discussion of the program's effectiveness.

Chapter 9 deals with public policy issues in the treatment of problem gambling. The recently issued recommendations of the National Gambling Impact Study Commission are summarized. Programs for the training and certification of problem gambling counselors are reviewed, as is the private gambling industry's response to problem gambling.

A "disclaimer" of sorts is needed before proceeding. Anyone who studies or writes about any aspect of gambling is likely to be asked at some point whether they think gambling is a good or bad thing. The author is neither for nor against the legalization of gambling or its expansion. The decision to gamble or not is a matter of individual choice. The only thing for which I am an advocate is the recognition of problem gambling as a very real but treatable disorder.

RONALD M. PAVALKO, Ph.D.

CONTENTS

PROBLEM GAMBLING AND ITS TREATMENT

Chapter 1

PROBLEM GAMBLING AS A
PSYCHIATRIC DISORDER

VARYING TERMINOLOGY: PATHOLOGICAL, COMPULSIVE, DISORDERED, AND PROBLEM GAMBLING

For the newcomer to the field of problem gambling, the variety of terms used to describe the disorder in which we are interested can be truly bewildering. During the past twenty-five years, researchers and clinicians have studied and talked about this disorder using terms inconsistently and using different terms interchangeably. The field has not yet reached complete consensus on precisely the term to be used and how to describe the degree to which this disorder is present.

An example can illustrate the situation. The professional organization that brings together people interested in problem gambling is called the National Council on Problem Gambling (NCPG). Formed in 1972, it was originally known as the National Council on Pathological Gambling. In the early 1990s the change from "pathological" to "problem" was intended to call attention to the wide range of problems that can be associated with gambling, not just "pathological" gambling. Most researchers and clinicians in the Unites States (and other countries) who are interested in this field of study or practice belong to the NCPG. In June 1999, 36 "state councils" were affiliated with the NCPG. The words these state councils use to identify themselves are interesting and important, because they reflect the lack of consensus on what term to use to describe this field. Half of the state councils use the term "problem gambling" in their official names. An additional 12 call themselves councils on "compulsive gambling," and four use both terms (problem and compulsive or compulsive and problem) in their official names. One calls itself a council on "gambling problems" and one is identified as a council on "problem gambling concerns." Of course, none of these names are inherently "right." The variation simply reflects the lack of consensus that exists.

Consequently, great care is needed when we try to compare the results of research addressing some aspect of problem gambling. Similarly, we cannot always be sure that clinicians or researchers using the same term (e.g., pathological) are talking about the same phenomenon, or that when different terms are used, the same phenomenon is not being referred to. Taking a careful look at how these terms are defined and what some of the differences are can reduce some of the confusion.

The American Psychiatric Association (APA) has shaped the evolution and development of the way in which this disorder is identified. The APA uses the term "pathological" gambling to describe this disorder. However, the terms "compulsive" and pathological gambling are often used interchangeably. Counseling professionals who treat problem gamblers tend to use the term pathological, because the APA regards pathological gambling as an "impulse control disorder" and not a "compulsion" (Lesieur, 1998).

The APA first recognized "pathological" gambling as a mental disorder in 1980 in the third edition of its *Diagnostic and Statistical Manual of Mental Disorders* (DSM III). In 1987 the APA published a revision of its Manual (DSM III-R) and identified nine criteria, at least four of which had to be present for a diagnosis of pathological gambling. These criteria follow very closely the criteria the APA uses to identify psychoactive substance dependence (alcohol, heroin, cocaine, and other drugs).

The fourth and most recent edition of this manual (DSM IV) was published in 1994. Ten criteria are used to define pathological gambling. According to the APA, a person must exhibit at least five of these criteria to be diagnosed as a pathological gambler . These criteria are presented in Table 1.2 and will be used later as a framework for developing an understanding of problem gambling (for a detailed analysis of how changes were made in the criteria, between DSM III-R and DSM IV, see Lesieur and Rosenthal, 1991).

TABLE 1.1
DSM IV DIAGNOSTIC CRITERIA FOR PATHOLOGICAL GAMBLING

1. Preoccupied with gambling (e.g., preoccupied with reliving past gambling experiences, handicapping, or planning the next venture, or thinking of ways to get money with which to gamble).
2. Needs to gamble with increasing amounts of money in order to achieve the desired excitement.
3. Repeated unsuccessful efforts to control, cut back, or stop gambling.
4. Restlessness or irritability when attempting to cut down or stop gambling.
5. Gambles as a way of escaping from problems or relieving dysphoric mood (e.g., feelings of helplessness, guilt, anxiety, or depression.
6. After losing money gambling, often returns another day in order to get even ("chasing one's losses).
7. Lies to family members, therapist, or others to conceal the extent of involvement with gambling.
8. Commits illegal acts such as forgery, fraud, theft or embezzlement to finance gambling.
9. Has jeopardized or lost significant relationship, job, or educational or career opportunity because of gambling.
10. Relies on others to provide money to relieve a desperate financial situation caused by gambling.

Source: Reprinted with permission from the *Diagnostic and Statistical Manual of Mental Disorders, Fourth Edition, Text Revision.* Copyright 2000, American Psychiatric Association, p. 674

"Disordered" gambling is another term that has been used to describe this disorder. In an extensive review of research on the prevalence of what has been called pathological, compulsive, and problem gambling, Shaffer, Hall, and Vander Bilt (1997) used the term "disordered gambling" to describe gambling that met the APA's criteria for pathological gambling. Operationally, disordered gambling is the same as pathological gambling.

The term "problem gambling" often gets used in two different ways. *First*, it is used to refer to gambling that leads to family, work, or financial problems but lacks the extreme characteristics of pathological gambling. In other words, "problem gambler" would be used to refer to people who have less serious problems than do pathological gamblers. *Second*, "problem gambling" also is used in a more inclusive way to capture a range of difficulties that people get into with gambling. This usage includes pathological gambling at one extreme and any problematic involvement with gambling at the other end of the continuum (Cox et al., 1997; Lesieur, 1998). A similarity exists here with the study of alcoholism. Although not all problem drinkers are alcoholics, those who are alcoholics certainly have a problem with drinking. The analogy would be that although not all problem gamblers are pathological gamblers, pathological gamblers clearly have a problem with gambling (Lesieur, 1998).

In the remainder of this book, we will use the terms "problem gambling" and "problem gambler" in this more inclusive way, except when the terms "pathological" or "compulsive" gambling are used in a quotation or paraphrased statement.

A FEW DEFINITIONS

The APA considers pathological gambling to be an impulse control disorder in which there is a chronic and progressive failure to resist impulses to gamble.

Compulsive/pathological gambling has also been described as "a progressive disorder characterized by a continuous or periodic loss of control over gambling; a preoccupation with gambling and with obtaining money with which to gamble; irrational thinking; and a continuation of the behavior despite adverse consequences" (Rosenthal and Lesieur, 1992).

One of the pioneers in the study of problem gambling, psychiatrist Robert Custer, defined "compulsive" gambling as "an addictive illness in which the subject is driven by an overwhelming uncontrollable impulse to gamble. The impulse progresses in intensity and urgency, consuming more and more of the individual's time, energy, and emotional and material resources. Ultimately, it invades, undermines, and often destroys everything that is meaningful in his life" (Custer and Milt, 1985:22).

USE, ABUSE, DEPENDENCE, AND ADDICTION

A good deal of conceptual confusion exits about the fundamental nature of problem gambling. Much of this confusion comes from the fact that the study of problem gambling has borrowed heavily from the study of alcohol and other drugs, and the confusion that exists in the "chemical dependency" literature has found its way into the study of gambling. Consequently, we need to look carefully at how the terms use, abuse, dependence, and addiction are used in the alcohol and other drug literature. Then we need to ask how these concepts apply to problem gambling.

Use and Abuse

One of the most serious points of confusion is the distinction between "use" and "abuse." Use really needs to be called "social use." The social use of drugs refers to the use of a drug in a social setting or context in which accepted cultural norms define it as appropriate. The use of a drug in religious ceremonies or family functions would be examples of such social use (Dowieko, 1999:13). What would the counterpart of this be for gambling? Gambling, especially card playing, is a commonplace activity at many family gatherings, as is playing bingo. In fact, many if not most people are introduced to gambling by parents and other family members. The placing of bets between friends and family members on sporting events or games of skill is also commonplace. The "friendly Friday night poker game" and "office pools" on sporting events are also activities that put gambling at the heart of social relationships between friends and coworkers. A level of culturally accepted "social gambling" seems to closely parallel the social use of drugs, even though about one in ten Americans is strongly opposed to any and all forms of gambling (Pavalko, 2000).

The least well-defined term in this area is drug "abuse." One leading expert on drugs has defined it as "the misuse of legal and illegal drugs" (Akers, 1992:15). In effect, "misuse" is substituted for "abuse" and leads to the question: "What is misuse?" Another defines it as "use of a drug by an individual when there is no legitimate medical need to do so. In the case of alcohol, the person is drinking in excess of accepted social standards" (Doweiko, 1999:13). Here, abuse boils down to use that deviates from (i.e., exceeds) accepted social and medical standards. A serious difficulty here is that "accepted standards" is a very broad and vague concept. Social standards regarding drug use vary considerable by region, community size, race and ethnicity, social class, education, religious affiliation, etc. As the history of drugs in American society shows, even medical standards regarding drug use have change considerably over time (Inaba and Cohen, 1989; Karch,

1998). As a final example of efforts to define abuse, consider this definition: "[abuse is] use of a drug in such a manner or in such amounts or in situations such that the drug use causes problems or greatly increases the chance of problems occurring" (Ray and Ksir, 1999:473). Although broad and comprehensive, this definition is at the same time very imprecise. It attempts to define abuse in terms of outcomes (problems) but raises obvious new questions, such as "What kinds of problems are we talking about?" "How severe does a situation have to be before it is a problem?" "Who defines when a problem exists (the user, a counselor) and what 'standards' do they use?" Given the murkiness of these definitions, we are really left with something akin to the problem of defining good art: its hard to define, but you know it when you see it. This is not a satisfactory way for empirical investigation to proceed.

Is there a gambling counterpart to the issue of drug abuse? The answer is a qualified "yes." When we talk about gambling becoming pathological, there is an implication that gambling per se is not an inherently harmful activity, but that pathological (or problem) gamblers are those who use the activity in an excessive, inappropriate way (i.e., they abuse it). Although the analogy is an appropriate one, all the difficulties that exist in defining drug abuse exist for defining "gambling abuse."

Dependence and Addiction

Another important issue is the distinction between dependence and addiction. Dependence really has two parts, physiological and psychological. When drugs are introduced into the body, changes that take place in tissues and cells as they adapt to the presence of the drug. *Physiological* dependence refers to the need for periodic doses of the drug to feel normal and function in a normal way. Tolerance and withdrawal are closely related to dependence. Tolerance refers to the need to increase the dosage to produce the same results, because the body becomes progressively immune to the effects of the drug. When the drug is not present in the body, we have a situation of disequilibrium or malfunctioning. This "abnormal" state is referred to as withdrawal. What has been referred to as "classic addiction" is the situation in which both tolerance and withdrawal are present (Goode, 1989).

Psychological dependence is a much less precise term used in several ways. Not all drugs produce physiological dependence (i.e., tolerance and withdrawal). Psychological dependence has been used to describe persistent, habitual drug taking behavior in which physiological dependence cannot be demonstrated or in which withdrawal symptoms are not severe. Psychological dependence has also been used to describe situations in which, in the absence of physiological dependence, drugs are taken because the person believes that they are needed (Dowieko, 1999:87).

How do the concepts of physiological and psychological dependence relate to problem and pathological gambling? With gambling, physiological dependence does not apply, because no substance is taken into the body. Yet, problem gamblers do exhibit behavior that is very similar to physiological dependence. Tolerance (gambling with increasing amounts of money and making bets with greater risk and return potential) and withdrawal (restlessness, irritability, and anxiety when unable to gamble) are both present. Psychological dependence is clearly present.

Addiction

Traditionally, the standard medical definition of addiction has focused on drugs: addiction is "the state of being given up to some habit, especially strong dependence on a drug." (Dorland, 1974). The addictive state is characterized by a) an overwhelming desire or need to use the drug and obtain it by any means, b) a tendency to increase the dosage (i.e., tolerance), c) psychological and usually physical dependence on the drug's effects, and d) a detrimental effect in the individual and society (Dorland, 1974). A broader definition moves the concept away from an exclusive focus on drugs: "an addiction exists when a person's attachment to a sensation, an object, or another person is such as to lessen his appreciation and ability to deal with other things in his environment or in himself so that he has become increasingly dependent on that experience as his only source of gratification" (Peele, 1979:56). In effect, addiction becomes "a way of life" (Cummings, 1979).

The concept of addiction poses a number of difficulties. Most of them are a result of the fact that, in the APA's DSM-IV, gambling is classified as "a disorder of impulse control," not as an addiction. The term "addiction" is limited to behavior associated with the use of chemical substances, despite the fact that problem gambling includes most of the classic characteristics of an addiction (Lesieur, 1989).

The meaning of the term "addiction," as used by the lay public, researchers, and clinicians has been seriously questioned and scrutinized in recent years. One leading researcher has argued that addiction is a lay term rather than a scientific concept and that "dependence" is a more appropriate term to use (Shaffer, 1999). Another has suggested that the term "addiction" be limited to physiological dependence, defining addiction as "the habitual daily use of a drug over time on which the person has developed physiological dependence" (Akers, 1992:22).

Problem gambling and other behaviors such as excessive shopping, game-playing, working, eating, having sex, and computer use have added a new dimension to the meaning of addiction. Although these are not physiological addictions, they fit the concept of a "psychological addiction." In recent discussions of addiction, such behaviors have been referred to as "activity" or "process" addictions.

Shaffer (1999) has proposed a scheme for identifying the possible presence of an addiction that bypasses the physiological/psychological dilemma and subsumes both activity and chemical dependence. Shaffer refers to the scheme as "the 3 Cs" because it includes a craving/compulsion dimension, continued involvement, and loss of control. In this scheme, addiction is evidenced by "Behavior that is motivated by emotions ranging along the Craving to Compulsion spectrum; craving can range from a mild desire to an overwhelming impulse to act. A compulsive behavior is a powerful repeating pattern of action. Continued involvement with the drug or activity in spite of adverse social, psychological, or biological consequences; Loss of Control, that is, a subjective sense that one no longer can control one's behavior" (Shaffer, 1999:13).

A more elaborate and comprehensive definition of addiction has been developed by Griffiths (1996, 2000). Addiction involves six core elements: salience, mood modification, tolerance, withdrawal, conflict, and relapse. The definition can apply to an activity (such as gambling) or to drug-taking behavior. *Salience* refers to a situation in which the activity becomes the most important thing in a person's life and dominates his or her thinking and feeling. *Mood modification* involves subjective experiences when engaged in the activity; these can be an aroused "high" or a tranquilizing escape or "numbness." *Tolerance* refers to the classic situation in which increasing amounts of the activity are needed to produce the desired mood modification. *Withdrawal* follows the standard definition too; it refers to unpleasant feeling states or physical effects when the activity is discontinued. *Conflict* involves conflicts with other people about the activity, conflict with other activities and interests, and conflict within the person such as feeling that one has lost the ability to control the activity. Finally, *relapse* refers to a return to high levels of the activity after efforts to control or abstain from it.

An important part of most definitions of addiction, including Shaffer's and Griffiths,' is "loss of control." The assumption is that the addict is unable to control the behavior in question, be it taking chemicals into the body or an activity such as gambling. Once established, loss of control is seen as permanent; this implies that the problem gambler will never be able to gamble without losing control, even after long periods of abstaining from gambling. The inability of chemical addicts to control their behavior has been seriously questioned by Schaler (2000). Citing research indicating that people who are heavy users of a variety of drugs are able to control their drug use and abstain altogether, Schaler essentially rejects the popular conception of addiction as a disease. His argument is similar to that of Fingarette (1988), who rejects the disease model of alcoholism largely on the basis of the control issue. Whether controlled gambling is possible is an unresolved issue to which we will return in discussing treatment in Chapter 7.

Why do some people become addicts but others do not? In an effort to answer this question and include addictions to activities (such as gambling), as well as drugs, Jacobs (1986) has made an important contribution to our understanding of addiction. According to Jacobs, there are two related predisposing factors. The *first* is an abnormal "physiological resting state" that is either excessively depressed or excessive excited. What this means is that a small proportion of the population experiences a persistent state of hypoarousal or hyperarousal. The assumption is that either of these states is stressful and predisposes such people to stress-reducing, potentially addictive substances and activities. The second predisposing factor is psychological in nature. It consists of experiences in childhood and adolescence that produce a deep sense of inadequacy. Experiences that lead a person to believe that he or she is inferior, unwanted, unneeded, or rejected by parents and others are painful. The assumption is that people make efforts to escape from such experiences and beliefs. When both these two factors are present, a high potential for addiction exists, but it remains latent unless the person encounters a substance or activity that provides an escape from these painful experiences. Jacobs argues that some addiction-prone people may go their entire lives without encountering an event that triggers addiction. Typically, addiction is triggered by a chance encounter with a substance or activity that produces a "Where have you been all of my life?" reaction and provides an escape from the pain.

Several studies have found empirical support for Jacob's theory. Martinez-Pina et al. (1991) found that adult pathological gamblers reported childhood feelings of rejection and inferiority and exhibited a higher prevalence of depression compared with a control group. Gupta and Derevensky (1998) also found abnormal physiological resting states and higher levels of emotional distress among adolescent problem and pathological gamblers compared with those without a gambling problem.

A final cautionary note about the concept of addiction is in order. We need to keep in mind that addiction is essentially a label we apply to a behavior. It is not an explanation of the behavior. Care needs to be taken not to confuse the definition with explanation. As Akers has pointed out, "We label excessive involvement in a drug [or activity] that the person cannot seem to give up as addiction, and think we have explained the excessive, hard-to-stop drug behavior [or activity] by saying that the person is suffering from an addiction. This says that addiction causes addiction" (Akers, 1992:21-22). Such tautological thinking can occur, because the addiction label implies that the behavior is beyond the person's control, but there is no independent way to confirm that the addict's behavior is not controllable (Shaffer, 1999:10).

THE MEDICAL MODEL

It is quite clear that problem gambling has become "medicalized," that is, it has come to be seen as a "disease," despite the fact that this way of viewing problem gambling has its critics (Blaszcsynski and McConaghy, 1989; Blume, 1987; Dickerson, 1987; Rosecrance, 1985). Consequently, physicians (mainly psychiatrists) and psychologists have developed a monopoly over the definition of the nature of problem gambling and the nature of the appropriate treatment for it.

The medical model is basically an explanation of (usually deviant) behavior that involves an *analogy* with physical illnesses. In other words, the explanation of the behavior is that the person exhibiting it does so because he or she has a "disease" and is "sick" (McGowan and Chamberlain, 2000). It is important to remember that even though it may be valuable to use this analogy, it does not mean that the problem gambler literally has a disease in the same way that a person may have a physical disease.

How does the medical model apply to problem gambling? Brown (1987) has pointed out that there are at least two variants of the medical model that have been used to explain problem gambling. One is that problem gambling is the result of a *genetic abnormality* that predisposes those with the abnormality to become problem gamblers. The analogy with drugs would be the argument of Alcoholics Anonymous that alcoholics have a genetically based allergy to alcohol. Another argument is that problem gambling is *a form of mental illness.* In this view, problem gambling is seen as an obsession or a compulsion with a loss of control over one's actions. The American Psychiatric Association's classification of "pathological" gambling as an "impulse control disorder" illustrates this variant (Brown, 1987).

Blume has added several points that explicate the meaning of the medical model. She regards it as an explanation for deviant behavior that locates its source within the individual and assumes that the behavior is the result of physiological, constitutional, or organic characteristics of the person interacting with the environment. Blume also points out the medical model does not imply that only physicians can treat the disorder, that the person with the illness is a passive actor, or that the disease has only a single cause. According to Blume, problem gambling has come to be regarded as an "addictive disease" because of its similarities with alcohol and other drug addiction (Blume, 1987).

Critiques of the Medical Model

Critiques of the medical model as an explanation of addiction generally, and problem gambling in particular, have been numerous.

Rosecrance (1985) has pointed out that the process of defining problem gamblers as "sick" reflects the consensus of clinicians but lacks any solid empirical basis.

Both Rosecrance (1985) and Castellani (2000) have pointed out that the medical model of problem gambling has gained acceptance largely because no competing explanations have been offered. Castellani (2000) examined in detail a 1983 trial in which a "compulsive gambler" charged with a $750,000 jewelry theft pleaded insanity. In rejecting this plea, the court also rejected the testimony of expert witnesses that compulsive gambling created a situation in which a person with the disorder could not be held responsible for his or her actions. Clearly, one difficulty with the medical model is that it raises the issue of responsibility for one's behavior. If one has a "sickness" (problem gambling) over which one has no control, the medical model implies that the behavior that results from that sickness is beyond one's control.

Castellani (2000) also points out that once problem gamblers have been labeled as "sick," they may try to use that label to their advantage. For example, they may try to get family members to excuse or forgive their behavior because of their illness. Furthermore, Castellani argues, because the medical model sees problem gambling as a matter of an individual pathological condition, treatment may ignore the needs and problems of members of the problem gambler's family.

The medical model's reliance on the disease analogy also promotes the idea that the person who has the disease in never "cured." In medical jargon, although signs of the disease may not be present, it is simply "in remission" and can re-emerge at any time. Problem gamblers who are not gambling are described as being "in recovery." Presumably, once identified as a "problem gambler," the label never goes away. This itself can be an obstacle to thinking of oneself and being seen by others as free of the disorder. A personal experience of the author illustrates this. At a national problem gambling conference in 1993, a well-known advocate for the treatment of problem gambling was introduced as "a recovering problem gambler." The man, then in his late sixties, prefaced his talk with the comment "Its been over 30 years since I gambled. I think its about time to call me a 'recovered' problem gambler." Members of the audience who were strong adherents of the disease concept of problem gambling could be heard muttering, "No, he's still recovering."

A final difficulty with applying the medical model to problem gambling involves the issue of whether diseases are dichotomous (i.e., either present or absent) or continuous (present to some degree). With most, but not all, physical illnesses there are clinical tests and criteria for determining whether a particular disease is present (i.e., a dichotomous determination). The same kind of clarity does not exist in the case of problem gambling. As we will see in our discussion of the assessment and diagnosis of problem gambling in Chapter 3, the "tests" for problem gambling reflect the fact that this disorder exists on a "continuous" scale, with the most recently developed assessment instrument distinguishing between "pathological," "problem," and "at-risk" gamblers. The determination of the presence of a gambling disorder is further complicated by the fact that it can wax and wane over time.

SUMMARY

Although the term "problem gambling" is used in this book, that choice is somewhat arbitrary, because a lack of consensus exits on what to call this disorder. The terms problem, compulsive, pathological, and disordered gambling are often used interchangeably, but have different meanings.

Use, abuse, dependence, and addiction are concepts used extensively in the study of chemical addiction. Although the status of problem gambling as an "addiction" is an unsettled issue, tolerance and withdrawal, the most basic features of addiction, are clearly present in problem gamblers. Various definitions of addiction have been proposed and serve as a useful guide to understanding problem gambling.

Clearly, thinking about problem gambling has been shaped by the "medical model" of deviant behavior, in which an analogy is made with physical "diseases." Although this model is useful, a number of valid criticisms of the model have been made.

REFERENCES

Akers, Ronald L.: *Drugs, Alcohol, and Society: Social Structure,Process, and Policy.* Belmont, CA: Wadsworth, 1992.

Blaszczynski, Alex, and McConaghy, Neil: The medical model of pathological gambling: Current shortcomings. *Journal of Gambling Behavior, 5*: 42-52, 1989.

Blume, Sheila B.: Compulsive gambling and the medical model. *Journal of Gambling Behavior, 3*:237-247, 1987.

Brown, R.I.F.: Models of gambling and gambling addictions as perceptual filters. *Journal of Gambling Behavior, 3*:224-236, 1987.

Castellani, Brian: *Pathological Gambling: The Making of a Medical Problem.* Albany: State University of New York Press, 2000.

Cox, Sue, Lesieur, Henry R., Rosenthal, Richard J., and Volberg, Rachel A.: *Problem and Pathological Gambling in America: The National Picture.* Columbia, National Council on Problem Gambling, January, 1997.

Cummings, N.A.: Turning bread into stones: Our modern antimiracle. *The American Psychologist, 34*:1119-1129, 1979.

Custer, Robert, and Milt, Harry: *When Luck Runs Out: Help for Compulsive Gamblers and Their Families.* New York: Facts on File, 1985.

Dorland: *Dorland's Illustrated Medical Dictionary,* 25th Ed. Philadelphia: W.B. Saunders, 1974.

Doweiko, Harold E.: *Concepts of Chemical Dependency,* 4th Ed. Pacific Grove, CA; Brooks/Cole, 1999.

Dickerson, Mark: The future of gambling research–learning from the lessons of alcoholism. *Journal of Gambling Behavior, 3*:248-256, 1987.

Fingarette, Herbert: *Heavy Drinking: The Myth of Alcoholism as a Disease.* Berkeley: University of California Press, 1988.

Goode, Erich: *Drugs in American Society,* 3rd Ed. New York, Knopf, 1989.

Griffiths, Mark D.: Nicotine, tobacco, and addiction. *Nature, 384*:18, 1996.

Griffiths, Mark D.: Internet addiction: Time to be taken seriously? Paper presented at the 14th National Conference on Problem Gambling, Philadelphia: October, 2000.

Gupta, Rina, and Derevensky, Jeffrey L.: An empirical examination of Jacob's *general theory of addictions*: Do adolescent gamblers fit the theory? *Journal of Gambling Studies, 14*:17-49, 1998.

Inaba, Darryl S., and Cohen, William E.: *Uppers, Downers, All Arounders.* Ashland, OR: Cinemed, Inc., 1989.

Jacobs, Durand F.: A general theory of addictions: A new theoretical model. *Journal of Gambling Behavior, 2*:15-31, 1986.

Karch, Steven B.: *A Brief History of Cocaine.* Boca Raton: CRC Press, 1998.

Lesieur, Henry R.: Current research into pathological gambling and gaps in the literature. In Shaffer, Howard J., and Stein, Sharon A., Gambino, Blase, and Cummings, Thomas N. (Eds.): *Compulsive Gambling: Theory, Research, and Practice.* Lexington: Lexington Books, 35-64, 1989.

Lesieur, Henry R.: Costs and treatment of pathological gambling. *The Annals, 556*: 153-171, March, 1998.

Lesieur, Henry R., and Rosenthal, Richard J.: Pathological gambling: A review of the literature (Prepared for the American Psychiatric Association task force on DSM-IV committee on disorders of impulse control not elsewhere classified). *Journal of Gambling Studies, 7*:5-39, Spring, 1991.

Martinez-Pina, A., Guirao de Parga, J.L., Fuste i Vallverdu, R., Serrat Planas, X., Martin Mateo, M., and Moreno Aguado, V.: The Catalonia survey: Personality and intelligence structure in a sample of compulsive gamblers. *Journal of Gambling Studies,* 7:275-299, 1991.

McGowan, William G., and Chamberlain, Linda L.: *Best Possible Odds: Contemporary Treatment Strategies for Gambling Disorders.* New York: Wiley, 2000.

Pavalko, Ronald M.: *Risky Business: America's Fascination With Gambling.* Belmont, CA: Wadsworth, 2000.

Peele, S.: Redefining addiction II: The meaning of addiction in our lives. *Journal of Psychedelic Drugs, 11:*289-297, 1979.

Ray, Oakley, and Ksir, Charles: *Drugs, Society, and Human Behavior,* 8th Ed. Boston: McGraw-Hill, 1999.

Rosecrance, John: Compulsive gambling and the medicalization of deviance. *Social Problems, 32:*275-284, 1985.

Rosenthal, Richard J. and Lesieur, Henry R.: Self-reported withdrawal symptoms and pathological gambling. *American Journal of Addictions, 1:*150-154, 1992.

Schaler, Jeffrey A.: *Addiction is a Choice.* Peru, IL: Open Court Publishing Company, 2000.

Shaffer, Howard J.: On the nature and meaning of addiction. *National Forum, 79:*9-14, 1999.

Shaffer, Howard J., Hall, Matthew N., and Vander Bilt, Joni: *Estimating the Prevalence of Disordered Gambling Behavior in   the United States and Canada: A Meta-Analysis.* Cambridge: MA: Harvard Medical School, December 15, 1997.

Chapter 2

PROBLEM GAMBLING AS AN ADDICTION

As indicated in Chapter 1, there is an unresolved debate about the basic nature of addiction and problem gambling as an addiction. Nevertheless, our understanding of problem gambling cannot wait for a resolution of that debate. Clinicians (i.e., counselors involved in diagnosing and treating problem gamblers) proceed on the assumption that problem gambling is an addiction and that problem gamblers exhibit many of the characteristics of chemically addicted people. In this chapter, the conventional perspective of clinicians on problem gambling as an addiction is summarized.

SIMILARITIES TO ALCOHOL AND OTHER DRUG ADDICTION

Problem gambling is not a physiological addiction like addiction to alcohol or other drugs, because no external substance is taken into the body. However, problem gamblers are seen as psychologically addicted or *psychologically* dependent on gambling (Walker, 1989).

Despite the difficulties that exist with the concept of addiction, the addiction analogy is used by clinicians to make sense of problem gambling. Problem gamblers exhibit behavior that makes the addiction analogy useful.

Dominance, Tolerance, and Withdrawal

The lives of problem gamblers are dominated by an intense *preoccupation* with gambling. This is quite similar to the way in which the lives of alcoholics and people addicted to other drugs are dominated by the quest for and consumption of drugs. Gambling is the focus of the problem gambler's life, typically to the exclusion of other interests. Problem gamblers gamble more often and with more money than they intend. They lose track of time when they are gambling, and they are unable to control the amount of money they gamble or the amount of time they spend gambling. It is not uncommon for problem gamblers to think they have spent an hour or two gambling even though they may have spent ten or twelve hours doing so. Even when not gambling, problem gamblers are planning the next venture or figuring out ways of obtaining money with which to gamble.

Like chemically addicted people, problem gamblers develop *tolerance.* As tolerance develops, they need to increase the amount they wager to achieve the desired excitement. They also escalate from simple to "exotic" wagers in which the risks and potential winnings are both great. Rather than a simple bet on a horse to win a race, they bet the daily double, quinellas, or trifectas. Rather than a simple "pass line" bet, the craps player takes the high risk-high payoff "proposition" bets in the center of the craps table layout.

Problem gamblers experience *withdrawal symptoms* when they attempt to limit or stop their gambling, similar to those experienced by chemically addicted people. When they can't get to a gambling venue, or when they do not have money with which to gamble, problem gamblers get irritable, nervous, angry, and restless.

DIFFERENCES FROM ALCOHOL AND OTHER DRUG ADDICTION

The similarities between problem gambling and addiction to alcohol and other drugs are striking, but some important differences exist.

Addiction to an Activity Rather than a Substance

Perhaps the most important difference is that problem gamblers are addicted to an activity rather than to a substance. Consequently, problem gambling is referred to as a "process addiction." Problem gamblers do not ingest, inject, or inhale chemical substances. Just what is it to which they become addicted? The answer seems to be "action." Action has been described in many ways. It is an aroused, euphoric state. It involves excitement, tension, and anticipation over the outcome of a gambling event. It is the thrill of living "on the edge," of having one's fate riding on the turn of a card, the roll of the dice, etc. Problem gamblers have described action as a "high" similar to that experienced from cocaine, heroin, or other drugs. Some report these sensations just thinking about, or anticipating a gambling activity, as well as when they are actually gambling. The tension and anticipation may build as they approach a casino or race track.

Problem gamblers also describe action as a "rush" that may include rapid heartbeat, sweaty palms, and even nausea. One problem gambler I talked with described his first big win ($600 on a longshot at the Arlington horse race track near Chicago) this way: "It was as if a bolt of lightning went off in my brain. Looking back [over a gambling career of 20 years], from that moment on, I was hooked. I keep trying to get that lightning bolt to go off again."

It is commonplace for problem gamblers to describe being in action as "better than drugs and better than sex." When they are in action, problem gamblers not only lose track of time, but ordinary physical needs take a back seat to the quest for action. They have been known to go for long periods of time (literally days) without sleep, food, water, or using a bathroom. Problem gamblers have also reported experiencing trance- like "disassociative" states in which they lose track of time and have "outer-body" experiences (Jacobs, 1989).

Counselor and Societal Perceptions

Another difference involves not the problem gambler or the addiction, but the way both are viewed by counselors, the human service system, and society at large.

Until very recently, counselors seeing clients for problems such as alcohol, other drugs, depression, and marital or relationship difficulties have typically not asked about the client's gambling behavior. Although counselors may inquire about and probe many facets of their client's personal lives, gambling has simply not been in their list of things to ask about. This is understandable. Problem gambling has not been a topic routinely covered in the professional education of counselors, and, consequently, they have not been very well informed about this disorder. Furthermore, very few public or private human service agencies have had gambling treatment experts on staff. There is a very slight likelihood that anyone seeing a counselor will be dealing with someone who knows very much about problem gambling.

The health insurance industry also treats problem gambling very differently than it treats chemical addiction. Put simply, in the United States there is no health insurance coverage for a *primary* diagnosis of problem (pathological) gambling. One promising development is that counselors in Employee Assistance Programs (EPAs) are beginning to show an interest in problem gambling, because they are seeing gambling problems in employees who seek their help for other problems. It is possible that EPAs will begin to demand that their health insurers cover treatment for problem gambling. Still, at the national level, the Americans with Disabilities Act specifically excludes gambling addicts from its coverage, while including those addicted to alcohol or other drugs.

Public understanding of problem gambling is also different from the way alcoholism has come to be viewed. All too often, many people regard the problem gambler as just a bad, stupid, or irresponsible person. During the past fifty years, the medical profession, the mass media, and self-help groups have slowly developed awareness among the general public that alcoholism and addiction to other drugs is a disease. Efforts to get problem gambling viewed as a "real" disorder are still in their infancy.

Behavior Limited Only by Access to Money

Unlike people addicted to alcohol and other drugs, problem gamblers can pursue their addictive behavior for as long as they have the financial resources to do so. In other words, the concept of "overdosing" in the case of chemical addiction has no counterpart in gambling addiction. The practical implication of this is that alcoholics and those addicted to other drugs can consume their drug to the point at which they do severe physical or mental damage to themselves or even kill themselves with an overdose. However, problem gamblers can continue gambling as long as they have access to money without ever "overdosing."

OTHER CHARACTERISTICS OF PROBLEM GAMBLING

In addition to the dominance, tolerance, and withdrawal discussed previously, problem gamblers exhibit several additional behaviors. When they lose, problem gamblers "*chase*" their loses in an effort to get even or win back what they have lost.   This is an extremely important characteristic that distinguishes recreational gamblers from problem gamblers (Lesieur, 1984). When they lose, most (nonaddicted, recreational) gamblers can rationalize their losses without further consequences. They may define their losses as the cost of their entertainment, or they may say that they chose to gamble rather than spend their money on an evening out to dinner, the theater, etc. Problem gamblers cannot do this. They make every effort to return as soon as they can (i.e., as soon as they have obtained more money) to try to win back what they have lost. Even when they win, problem gamblers cannot stop. A win simply spurs them on to try to get more and bigger wins. This does not occur because of a desire to win money as an end in itself. Rather, money is essential to stay in action.

McCown and Keiser (2000) conducted a study that provides some insight into the chasing process. Two groups of subjects were given unlimited access to imaginary quarters to play slot machines. The machines of one group were set to pay off, on average, at 83 percent; the other groups' machines were set to pay off at 95 percent. Of course, the group playing the low payoff machines lost their money quicker. Once their initial stake (1,000 "quarters") was lost, they tended to play with more vigor and at a faster pace, compared with those playing the higher payoff machines. They also began placing multiple bets in an attempt to compensate for what they had lost. In effect, the more they lost, the more rapidly they "chased" their losses in an effort to get even. It should be noted that the subjects were not problem gamblers.

Problem gamblers also *lie to family and friends* about their gambling activities, their losses, and their gambling debts. They go to great lengths to attempt to keep their gambling, their losses, and their gambling debts a secret as long as possible. They construct elaborate lies and charades to conceal their activities and related problems. The lengths to which problem gamblers will go to conceal the scope of their gambling and money problems (especially from a spouse) is truly remarkable. They have been known to rent secret post office boxes so that notices from bill collectors or credit card statements do not come to their home, use fictitious names on bank accounts and loans, and hide extra money in their shoes or their cars when going to a gambling venue with a spouse or other people. They become very skilled at maintaining the fiction that their gambling is a harmless and casual recreational activity.

Compulsive gamblers *borrow money* from friends, relatives, coworkers, banks, loan companies, credit unions, credit cards, loan sharks, etc. to pay their gambling debts and stay in action. The average gambling-related debt of male compulsive gamblers has been estimated between $42,000 and $54,000 in several studies, excluding home mortgages, car loans, and other consumer loans (Council on Compulsive Gambling of New Jersey, 1991). The level of indebtedness is approximately one-third lower for female compulsive gamblers.(Lesieur, 1988).

Given their indebtedness and the desire to stay in action, it is not surprising that problem gamblers will engage in a variety of *criminal behaviors.* When opportunities present themselves or when their financial situation becomes desperate, problem gamblers engage in illegal activities to obtain money with which to gamble or to pay off gambling debts. They eventually become mired in a cycle of indebtedness in which they are constantly seeking funds to pay off their debts and continue their gambling.

About two- thirds of members of Gamblers Anonymous report that they have engaged in illegal activities to pay gambling debts or obtain money with which to gamble (National Council on Problem Gambling, n.d.). The illegal activities reported include forgery, embezzlement, fraud, tax evasion/fraud, and a variety of "street crimes."

The commission of crimes by problem gamblers is often a matter of opportunity and interpersonal contacts. For example, those who bet on races and sporting events with illegal bookies may become bookies themselves or become "runners" for bookies to obtain gambling money or pay off gambling debts (Lesieur, 1984).

In three studies of members of Gamblers Anonymous that included a total of 394 people in Illinois, Wisconsin, and Connecticut, 56.6 percent admitted to stealing in various ways to finance their gambling (summarized in Lesieur, 1998a). The total amount of money stolen by these 394 people was $30,065,812, for an average of $76,309. One had stolen $8 million, and another had stolen $7.5 million.

Another study of 306 Australian problem gamblers found that 59 percent had committed at least one gambling-related crime during his or her gambling career. The most common crimes were larceny, embezzlement, misappropriation of funds, breaking and entering, and shoplifting. Armed robbery, drug dealing, and other crimes were less frequently reported (Blaszcznski and McConaghy, 1994).

When the criminal activities (especially theft of money or embezzlement) of problem gamblers are detected, it is not unusual for them to say that they were "just borrowing" the money with the intention of using it to gamble with and returning it from their winnings. This may sound like a lame effort to avoid arrest, but it occurs so often that it must be given some credibility, at least for what it tells us about how problem gamblers think. They believe so strongly that they can and will win, that a "big score" is just around the corner and will take care of all their problems, that the idea of temporarily "borrowing" someone else's money and returning it before it is missed seems quite reasonable to them.

Problem gamblers also have a high incidence of *stress related* disorders such as insomnia, intestinal disorders, and migraine headaches. There is an especially high incidence of depression. Studies of members of Gamblers Anonymous have found that between 70 and 76 percent of them have been diagnosed with depression by a mental health professional at some time in their lives (Lesieur, 1998b). Depression also was found to be significantly higher among members of Gamblers Anonymous compared with a control group of nonproblem gamblers (Getty et al., 2000). Whether they gamble to relieve depression (as the DSM IV criteria suggest) or whether depression is a result of their gambling-related problems (indebtedness, marital conflicts, job loss) is an unresolved issue.

Studies of members of Gamblers Anonymous, problem gamblers in treatment, and others have dealt with attempted *suicide* as a result of gambling problems. This research is summarized in Table 2.1. In all cases, these attempted suicide rates are considerably higher than the attempted suicide rate in the general population.

TABLE 2.1
ATTEMPTED SUICIDE RATES AMONG PROBLEM GAMBLERS: A SUMMARY

Study	Location	Population	Attempted Suicide Rate
Frank, Lester, & Wexler	U.S.	GA Members	13%
McCormick, Russo, Ramirez, & Taber	U.S.	Gamblers seeking treatment	12%
Schwarz & Lindner	Germany	Gamblers seeking treatment	31%
Horodecki	Austria	Pathological gamblers seeking treatment	8%
Moran	U.K.	Pathological gamblers	20%
Bland, Newman, Orn, & Stebelsky	Canada	Pathological gamblers	13%
Ladouceur, Dube, & Bujold	Canada	College student pathological gamblers	27%
Sullivan	New Zealand	Gamblers calling helpline	4%

Sources: Frank, Michael L., Lester, David, and Wexler, Arnold: Suicidal behavior among members of Gamblers Anonymous. *Journal of Gambling Studies, 7:*249-253, 1991; McCormick, R., Russo, A., Ramirez, L., and Taber, J.: Affective disorders among pathological gamblers seeking treatment. *American Journal of Psychiatry, 141:*215-218, 1984; Schwarz, Jurgen, and Lindner, Andreas: Inpatient treatment of male pathological gamblers in Germany. *Journal of Gambling Studies. 8:*93-107, 1992; Horodecki, Izabela: The treatment model of the guidance center for gamblers and their relatives in Vienna/Austria. *Journal of Gambling Studies, 8:*115-129, 1992; Moran, J.: Taking the final risk. *Mental Health,* Winter, 21-22, 1969; Bland, R., Neuman, S., Orn, H., and Steblesky, B.: *Canadian Journal of Psychiatry, 38:*108-112, 1993; Ladouceur, R., Dube, D., and Bujold, A.: Prevalence of pathological gambling and related problems among college students in the Quebec metropolitan area. *Canadian Journal of Psychiatry, 39:*289-293, 1994; and Sullivan, S.: Why compulsive gamblers are a high suicide risk. *Community Mental Health in New Zealand, 8:*40-47, 1994.

In addition to actually attempting suicide, problem gamblers have been asked about the extent to which they have thought about or considered suicide. This is referred to as "suicidal ideation." Suicidal ideation rates of 17, 21, and 30 percent were found in three U.S. studies (Frank, Lester, and Wexler, 1991; Lesieur and Blume, 1990; and McCormick et al., 1984). In other societies, suicidal ideation rates of 35 percent (Germany), 70 percent (Austria), and 80 percent (New Zealand) have been reported (Horodecki, 1992; Schwarz and Lindner, 1992; and Sullivan, 1994). It is also more than a coincidence that the suicide rate in Nevada is the highest of any state in the country and about twice the national average (U.S. Bureau of the Census, 1999).

PROBLEM GAMBLING AS A HIDDEN ADDICTION

Because problem gambling is an addiction to an activity rather than a substance, it is much more difficult to detect and easier to conceal than is chemical addiction. The absence of physical signs of addiction makes it easier to conceal from friends, family members, and counselors. You can't smell problem gambling on a problem gambler's breath. A problem gambler's eyes don't dilate. Dice, chips, and cards don't leave marks on a problem gambler's arms. Problem gambling doesn't make you walk funny, stagger, or fall down in a stupor the way excessive alcohol consumption can. Consequently, it is often referred to as a "hidden addiction" (Pavalko, 1999).

As already noted, awareness of problem gambling is not very extensive among professional counselors. They may be dealing with problem gamblers, treating them for other problems, and never ask about the client's gambling activities. Very few members of Gamblers Anonymous report that they were referred there by a mental health professional. Those who have been treated by psychiatrists, psychologists, and other counselors for mental health problems report that they were rarely asked about their gambling behavior. This also contributes to keeping problem gambling a hidden addiction.

PERSONALITY CHARACTERISTICS OF THE
PROBLEM GAMBLER

If there is a "problem gambling personality type," it has yet to be identified in a precise manner. However, problem gamblers do exhibit some distinctive characteristics. Although these are commonly found among problem gamblers, it must be remembered that not every problem gambler will exhibit all of them or exhibit them in an extreme way. There is considerable "diversity" among problem gamblers. Some are "action seekers" drawn to gambling for the excitement it offers. Others are "escape gamblers" who use gambling as an escape from a variety of personal problems.

Problem gamblers tend to be very intelligent, energetic, hard working people who enjoy challenging tasks (e.g., handicapping races or sporting events). They also tend to be narcissistic, arrogant, and very self-confident (Taber et al., 1986). After all, they believe that they have the power to beat the laws of probability. They see themselves as "winners" and others as "losers" or "suckers." Ironically, they also value the attention and recognition that comes from being perceived as a winner by others.

They also have a need to control events. Gambling provides the illusion that they can control the uncontrollable. Some develop a kind of "irrational thinking" in which they come to believe that they can (literally) control the turn of a card, the roll of the dice, the spin of a wheel, or the outcome of a race. In the advanced stages of this disorder, especially when they see their financial problems as unsolvable and they become desperate, problem gamblers begin thinking backward about their problems. Rather than seeing their financial, family, work, legal, and other problems as a *result* of their gambling, they see further gambling as the *solution* to their problems. "If only I had money to gamble with, I could win more money and all my problems would be taken care of" is the all too familiar complaint of the problem gambler. There is no financial problem so great that it can't be solved by more gambling an the "inevitable" win.

Evidence also exists that problem gamblers are self-centered, insecure, and tend to exhibit a disregard for authority. They are highly competitive but seem to have abandoned or given up on conventional ways of competing. The interpretation is that, having doubts about the strength of their personal resources to compete in conventional ways, gambling becomes a way of trying to be successful (Graham and Lowenfeld, 1986). This perspective is consistent with Merton's (1957) idea that when people do not have access to conventional and socially approved means for achieving success, they will become "innovative" and turn to deviant means of achieving the goal of success.

CROSS ADDICTION AND ADDICTION SWITCHING

Additional support for the idea that problem gambling is an addiction comes from evidence that chemical dependency and problem gambling are related (Cunningham-Williams et al., 2000). There are two different processes involved: cross addiction and addiction switching.

Cross Addiction

Research on members of Gamblers Anonymous and compulsive gamblers in treatment has found that between 47 and 52 percent have had a serious chemical addiction (usually alcohol) at some point in their lives and frequently for a long period of time (Lesieur, 1998b). In addition, studies of people being admitted to or receiving inpatient treatment for alcohol and other drug addiction have found that between 9 and 19 percent are problem gamblers (Lesieur, 1984 and 1998b; Lesieur et al., 1986; Lesieur and Heineman, 1988; Lesieur and Rosenthal, 1991).

A Canadian study also provides evidence of a link between gambling and other addictions. This study of 2,016 adults found that heavy gamblers were more likely to binge drink and smoke than were light and moderate gamblers or nongamblers (Smart and Ferris, 1996). Another study of 61 self-identified problem gamblers found that 24 percent were problem drinkers and an additional 8 percent had problems with other drugs (Coyle and Kinney, 1990).

Several studies of college students have also documented a connection between problem gambling and the use of alcohol and other drugs. Ladoucuer et al. (1994) found that 2.8 percent of 1,471 Quebec (Canada) college students were probable pathological gamblers. Pathological gambling was directly related to tobacco use, alcohol abuse, and frequency and number of illegal drugs used. Lesieur et al.'s study of 1,771 university students in five states found that between 4 percent (Nevada) and 8 percent (New York) were probable pathological gamblers. Pathological gamblers were more likely than other students to abuse alcohol and other drugs (Lesieur, et al., 1991). In the mid-1990s, a study of 835 college students in Reno and Memphis found that about 25 percent of the students who gamble in casinos drink alcohol while gambling either frequently or always. Among men, those who drank while gambling were more likely than non-drinkers to bet more money, obtain additional money while at the casino, and lose more than they felt they could afford. These relationships were not found among women who drank while gambling (Giacopassi et al., 1998).

Another study of 1,051 patients seeking help for medical problems (having nothing to do with gambling) at three primary care clinics in Wisconsin also found evidence of a connection between problem gambling and alcohol consumption, cigarette smoking, and marijuana use. Compared with patients who did not have a gambling problem, problem gamblers were more likely to be heavy consumers of alcohol, tobacco, and marijuana (Pasternak and Fleming, 1999).

Addiction Switching

Besides cross addiction, addiction switching also occurs. The evidence on this consists mainly of the reports of counselors who have found that about 10 percent of recovering alcoholics replace their alcohol use with gambling, and about the same proportion of recovering problem gamblers become heavy consumers of alcohol (Blume, 1994).

THE COURSE OF THE ADDICTION: WINNING, LOSING, AND DESPERATION

The development of problem gambling usually follows a typical sequence, originally identified by Custer and Milt (1985). The sequence includes three stages: winning, losing, and desperation. In the *winning phase,* occasional gambling often includes frequent winning experiences and is accompanied by increased excitement about gambling, more frequent gambling, and increased amounts of money being wagered. The early gambling careers of problem gamblers usually include a "big win." This creates unreasonable optimism and fantasies about continuing to win big. The big win also serves as a "baseline" for the future. As losses inevitably occur, the gambler "knows" he or she can win big, because it has happened before. The winning phase also includes bragging about how much one is winning, thinking about gambling to the exclusion of other things, and a feeling of being invulnerable.

Wins cannot continue indefinitely. It is inherent in the basic principles of commercial gambling (especially casino games) that the laws of probability and the house advantage built into the games catch up with the gambler. Wins may continue to occur, but losses overshadow them. As gamblers enter the losing phase, there are prolonged losing episodes in which the gambler chases losses, "knows" that a big win is just around the corner, and simply cannot stop gambling. They begin borrowing from friends, relatives, banks (second mortgages, personal loans), taking credit card advances, and taking markers (short-term loans) from casinos. Gamblers neglect family responsibilities, delay paying bills and debts, lose time from work, and lie about their gambling and their losses. Personality changes, including irritability and restlessness, and depression occur.

Gamblers enter the *desperation phase* as their ability to pay bills and loans becomes more difficult. Their borrowing becomes heavier, and they may turn to loan sharks and bookies. They become increasingly alienated from friends and family who, having been "burned" many times, refuse to bail them out. Toward the end of this phase, gambling becomes more frantic, and gambling-related problems dominate the gambler's life. At this point, they may commit crimes to get money. They begin blaming others for their problems (especially those who won't loan them money), which exacerbates their alienation and isolation. Hopelessness, suicidal thoughts and attempts, arrest, divorce, alcohol problems, emotional breakdowns, and withdrawal symptoms all can be part of the end of the desperation phase.

This sequence of phases is a general pattern. The problem gambling careers of particular individuals may not involve all the characteristics included in each phase, and the rate at which they move through each phase can vary.

It is also likely that this general, typical pattern will not always apply to all segments of the population. In particular, some of the specific elements of this process may not apply to adolescents and elderly people. For example, to the extent that they are isolated from or do not have friends and relatives to borrow money from, the amount and extent of borrowing among older people may be less than for younger people. Adolescents may also lack easy access to credit, for example, by virtue of not having credit cards or property that can be used as collateral for loans.

The work-related difficulties that are part of the process would not be relevant to older people who are retired. In the case of adolescents, problems may show up in school that are the counterpart of work problems. Because many of the crimes committed by problem gamblers to get money are work-related "white collar" crimes, retired people would not have the opportunity to commit them, although forgery and tax and insurance fraud would still be options. Similarly, adolescents would be less likely than young adults or middle-aged people to have jobs that provided them with the opportunity commit these white collar crimes.

ACTION AND ESCAPE GAMBLERS

The distinction between action and escape gamblers was noted earlier and requires additional comment. Until very recently, much of our image of the problem gambler was based on information from members of Gamblers Anonymous, who typically have been older men with long histories of gambling. These generally have been action gamblers involved in betting on horse races and sporting events and playing casino games such as blackjack and craps. Excitement, anticipation of an outcome, the thrill of making a high-risk/high-return wager all drive the action gambler.

The use of gambling as an escape has been recognized for some time. However, the use of the term "escape gambler" is relatively recent. In this case, the experience of counselors working with problem gamblers is the basis for the term and the distinction between action and escape gamblers.

These two types of gamblers–action and escape–are in all likelihood related to different personality characteristics that problem gamblers exhibit. Those with "narcissistic" personalities also tend to be self-centered, easily frustrated, impatient, and demanding. They tend to be attracted to competitive games and those that require skill (e.g., handicapping races or sporting events), and they are likely to have fantasies about being big winners (Rosenthal and Rugle, 1994). Escape gamblers, on the other hand, are more likely to be introverted, depressed, and avoidant. They use gambling to escape from feelings of hopelessness and helplessness (Kruedelbach et al., 1999; McCormick and Taber, 1988; Lesieur and Rosenthal, 1991).

As legal commercial gambling has expanded, it has attracted new gamblers–people who previously would not want to get involved in illegal gambling, who found handicapping races and sporting events too complex and demanding, or who found table games like blackjack and craps intimidating. The expansion of commercial casino gambling has been largely an expansion of machine games–slot machines and video poker machines. And the new gamblers attracted to them have been primarily women. Slot and video poker machines offer a marvelous escape. Unlike handicapping, blackjack, or craps, playing slot machines requires absolutely no skill. One can simply put in coins or tokens, push a button, and get an outcome. Although video poker requires some skill, in the form of decisions to be made, if one makes a mistake (a wrong decision), the machine doesn't care. It doesn't chastise or criticize you the way another player might at a blackjack table. For the person who wants to escape from their problems, the machines are the place to be. They are the escape gambler's nirvana. What kinds of things are escape gamblers escaping from? The list is as long as the list of human problems and concerns: abuse, an alcoholic spouse, a disappointing or unsatisfactory relationship, loneliness, isolation, the death of a spouse or other family member, work problems, legal problems, etc.

Unfortunately, we have no solid, empirical data on the number or proportion of action and escape gamblers in the general gambling population. Likewise, we do not know in any precise way what proportion of problem gamblers are action and escape gamblers.

On the basis of experiential information from counselors, it is possible to paint a tentative, general portrait of action and escape gamblers. *Action gamblers* are more likely to be men who started gambling at a relatively young age. Some evidence exists that, for men, gambling is a form of self-enhancement and self-expression, but it does not have this meaning for women (Jang et al., 2000). This is consistent with the general images of action and escape gamblers. Action gamblers also tend to be highly competitive and have a number of gambling friends, to whom they like to brag about their winnings. They also tend to be highly narcissistic, act like "big shots," and be heavy tippers. Compared with escape gamblers, action gamblers are more likely to have engaged in criminal activity and have an arrest record. Late in their gambling careers they may gamble even more to try to solve the financial problems that have accumulated over time as a result of their gambling.

Escape gamblers are more likely to be women who began gambling much later in life than action gamblers. By the time they become problem gamblers, they have had a comparatively short gambling career. For the escape gambler competition is relatively unimportant. Rather than being a competitive activity, gambling is an emotional reaction to whatever personal or relationship issues they are trying to escape from. Lesieur and Blume (1991) report that female gamblers are more likely than male gamblers to use gambling as a way of avoiding or getting relief from relationship problems. A female gambler's comments illustrate this: "I went out gambling when my husband was drunk so we wouldn't fight...and the money I had gave me the time–the time away, the time of not thinking, the time of not worrying" (Lesieur and Marks, 1993). The indebtedness of escape gamblers also is usually less than that of action gamblers. Again, it needs to be stressed that this is a preliminary characterization of action and escape gamblers that needs to be confirmed and possibly modified by additional empirical research.

SECURITIES TRADING: AN OVERLOOKED FORM OF GAMBLING

Most discussions of gambling are limited to conventional forms of gambling such as betting on horse or dog races and sporting events, playing the lottery and bingo and, of course, casino games. Indeed, to this point, our discussion of gambling has assumed that we are dealing with these kinds of activities. However, it is appropriate to think of certain kinds of commonplace business activities as a form of gambling. In particular, the trading of stocks, bonds, futures, and options have many parallels with more conventional gambling.

FUTURES AND OPTIONS

A *future* is a contract to buy a particular commodity, such as a stock index. It is essentially a bet that the price of the index will rise or fall. If the price moves in the direction you have predicted, you can sell the option at a profit. An *option* is basically a bet on the value of a futures contract. You can bet that the price will rise (known as a "call") or that it will fall (known as a "put"). In either case, you own a piece of paper that is a bet on the future value of another piece of paper (the futures contract). In general, the prices of options on futures swing more widely than the prices of options on the stock indexes. Futures and options are highly speculative investments that carry high risks and the potential for high returns. In a sense, it is a very "pure" form of gambling. Similar to betting on horse races, one is not betting against the "house" (e.g., casino) but against the other players (for further discussion of futures and options see Fabozzi and Kipnis, 1989; Quinn, 1991). Some people who engage in such trading are essentially problem gamblers. Unfortunately, we know very little about their numbers or their social characteristics.

What such trading activities have in common with gambling is that they both involve risk taking, and the relationship between risk and return is essentially the same. High-risk bets (purchases) can lead to high returns and low-risk bets (purchases) can produce low returns. It is significant that the language of the securities markets and the world of conventional gambling have many similarities. Securities traders talk of "beating the market," and "hedging their bets." A profitable investment may be referred to as "a gamble that paid off."

Does this mean that everyone who invests in stocks or bonds is a "gambler?" Not at all. It is important to make a distinction between "investing" and "trading." This distinction is not always an easy one to make. The line between the two is hazy rather than clear. *Investing* involves purchasing something (usually a stock or bond) with the idea of holding it for a considerable length of time (usually a year or more) and with the hope of selling it at a profit, but often holding it indefinitely. *Trading*, on the other hand, refers to buying securities in a much shorter timeframe (days, weeks, hours, minutes). As a much more active, intense, and short-term effort to turn a profit, trading is very similar to conventional forms of gambling. A great deal of popular, media attention has been given to "day trading" in recent years. This involves the making of high-speed purchases and sales using the Internet. Day trading isn't really all that new. Before the advent of the internet, a trader simply called a broker to make the transactions. What is new is the speed with which transactions can be made.

One writer for a financial magazine has described these kinds of traders as measuring their goals in hours, looking up the value of their portfolios first thing in the morning and being unable to go an hour without checking it, having nightmares and cold sweats if they miss a price trigger alert, and unable to wait for "after hours" trading after the close of the New York Stock Exchange and the NASDAQ (Fredman, 1999). In effect, securities trading dominates their lives in much the same way gambling dominates the lives of problem gamblers. Another financial commentator has basically equated day trading with "online gambling" and, in particular, compared buying on margin (i.e., buying with money borrowed from a broker) to gambling with a loan from a casino (Cruz, 1999).

As indicated earlier, very little systematic data exists on the topic of gambling in the securities market, and no solid research exist on the topic. However, two personal experiences provide some insight into the process. The experiences of a recovering problem gambler (who also treats problem gamblers) are illustrative of the dynamics of gambling in the securities markets. As a stockbroker who had never placed a bet on a conventional gambling game, the trading of stock options was his form of gambling, placing huge amounts of money at risk and, eventually, losing it all. On the basis of his experiences and those of others, he has identified several indicators that securities trading may be shading into gambling. One is trading for the "action" of it, in which the trader is less concerned about the money than the excitement of the deal. Another indicator is trying to "catch up" with the market. For example, if one missed yesterday's market rise and feels that it is essential to win big today to make up for yesterday's lost opportunity, or if one lost money yesterday and must make it up today, the strategy is similar to "chasing one's losses." Trading with borrowed money, especially to follow up on a hot tip also indicates a change in behavior that is more like a gambler than an investor. Investors, like gamblers, have a "system" or strategy that they follow. Not sticking with the system when one is losing and making unsuitable purchases or sales is another sign of gambling rather than investing. A final indicator is purchasing securities with money that one can't afford to lose because one is sure that the next purchase is going to be a "big winner" (Jaffe, 1999).

Another personal experience has been reported by a man with a doctoral degree who was an options trader over a thirty-year period. During that time, he reports losing more than $670,000. He also reports being fired from three professional jobs (including college teaching) because of absenteeism and unreliability as a result of his gambling in the options market. One episode during a trading career is similar to what happens to problem gamblers generally. During a six-week period, he tripled a $10,000 investment only to lose it all plus another $7,000 in one day. In reflecting on his behavior while trading options, he recounts many experiences similar to those of the typical problem gambler: a focus on his trading to the exclusion of everything else (including his job), stress-related physical symptoms (shortness of breath, tightness in chest, unsteadiness), fatigue, concealment of his trading activities from family members, and an inability to leave the computer monitor displaying trading information (despite, on occasion, extreme physical discomfort because of the need to go to the bathroom) (Steinberg and Harris, 1994).

GAMBLING ON THE INTERNET

The trading of securities, and especially "day trading," can and does involve the use of the internet, and internet trading and investing have become commonplace. However, there is another important way in which the internet is involved in gambling and, potentially, problem gambling. Since making their first appearance in 1995 (Christensen and Cummings, 1995), online "virtual" casinos and sports books have grown phenomenally. In January 2001, the author went to the internet site "Internetcasinolist.com" and found 687 online, internet casinos listed. About 200 of these also offered betting on sporting events. In March of 2000, a similar exercise produced a count of 283 such casinos (Pavalko and Teske, 2000). Such sites are constantly being added, others go out of business, and the number fluctuates a great deal. In January of 2001, a study of Internet gambling sites by Christiansen Capital Advisors and the River City Group, two companies that follow developments in the gambling industry, identified 1,400 "gaming sites" (Schneider, 2001). This larger number probably includes casinos, casinos with sports books, sports books only, and government-operated lotteries located outside the United States.

Internet gambling sites are illegal in the United States. They operate mainly out of Caribbean countries, where they are licensed but unregulated. Given the absence of regulation, it is difficult to identify with any precision how many people gamble at them and how much money is being wagered. However, estimates have been made that hint at the scope of internet gambling. For example, one sports book called "Interops.com," based in Antigua, reported that it took 875,000 bets on U.S. football games during the 1998 season and more than1 million bets during the 1999 season before the NFL playoffs began. They estimated that they would accept at least 92,000 bets on the 2000 Super Bowl (Jesdanun, 2000). Another indicator of the scope of Internet gambling is the gross revenues (the amount bet minus the amount paid back to the players) that gambling sites earn. For 1998, this was estimated at $651 million (Schauerte, 1999) and $811 million for 1999 (Green, 1999). One person who follows this segment of the gambling industry estimates that gross revenues will be $10 billion by 2003 (Green, 1999).

Internet gambling has the potential to make gambling accessible to people regardless of the distance they live from a "bricks and mortar" casino. It can be very attractive to many people for a number of reasons. People with physical limitations and disabilities can gamble online from their homes. Bad weather need not be a deterent to playing casino games. Once an account with an internet casino has been established, credit card and ATM accounts can be used to place bets. Betting from home is a way for nonsmokers to avoid the ever-present cloud of smoke that fills most casinos. And people with children do not need to worry about arranging care for their children while they are gambling.

In January 2001, the American Psychiatric Association (APA) issued an warning about some of the hazards of internet gambling. Concern was expressed about the fact that internet gambling is a solitary activity in which people can gamble uninterrupted and undetected for unlimited periods of time, thereby increasing the potential for addiction. The APA's warning also noted that many (nongambling) "game" sites used by children and adolescents have links to gambling sites, thereby encouraging and making it easy for young people to access gambling sites (American Psychiatric Association, 2001).

Does internet gambling have a greater or lesser potential for the development of gambling problems than other, more conventional gambling venues? No one knows for sure, but there is every reason to believe that it can be as addictive as any other form of gambling. Once connected to an internet service provider (ISP) and having established an account, a person can be playing casino games or placing bets on sporting events within minutes. Internet gambling provides opportunities for very rapid play. For example, one can play a blackjack hand every few seconds, much faster that at a casino blackjack table, where there is "dead time" as other players are dealt their cards, money is collected and bets paid, players exchange money for chips, and cards get shuffled. Consequently, losses can mount more rapidly than at a conventional casino game. Given the way internet casino gambling has grown since it first appeared in 1995, and growth projections for the future, this form of gambling can be expected to produce at least its proportionate share of problem gamblers.

SUMMARY

Although problem gambling is similar in many ways to chemical addiction (dominance, tolerance, and withdrawal), there are also important differences. Problem gambling is an addiction to an activity rather than a substance. Problem gamblers become addicted to "action." Societal (and counselors) perceptions of problem gambling are different, and the possibility of "overdosing" does not exist with problem gambling.

Problem gamblers "chase" their losses, lie to other people about the extent of their gambling and gambling-related problems, and go to great lengths to conceal their gambling activities and indebtedness. They may engage in criminal behavior (especially white collar crimes) to support their gambling and have a high rate of attempted suicide and stress-related disorders. The careers of problem gamblers follow a predictable sequence, as they move from the winning to the losing, and finally the desperation phase. It is important to distinguish between action and escape gamblers; the former gamble for the excitement, whereas the latter gamble as a way of escaping from or avoiding a variety of personal problems.

The trading of securities, a fundamental part of the American business scene, shares many characteristics with gambling, and some of the riskier forms of trading have a potential for addiction similar to that of many "conventional" forms of gambling. Gambling has also become readily available on the internet, where sports betting is offered along with conventional casino games. Given the newness of internet gambling, its impact on problem gambling is difficult to assess, but it seems to have the same if not a greater potential for addiction than other forms of gambling.

REFERENCES

American Psychiatric Association: APA advisory on internet gambling. *Health Advisory.* Washington, DC: American Psychiatric Association, January 16, 2001.

Blaszczynski, Alex and McConaghy, Neil: Criminal offenses in Gamblers Anonymous and hospital treated pathological gamblers. *Journal of Gambling Studies, 10:* 99-127, Summer, 1994.

Blume, Sheila B.: Pathological gambling and switching addictions: report of a case. *Journal of Gambling Studies, 10:*87-96, Spring, 1994.

Christensen, Eugene Martin, and Cummings, Will E.: Gross annual wager: 1994. *International Gaming and Wagering Business, 16:* 29-76, August 1, 1995.

Council on Compulsive Gambling of New Jersey: 1-800 hotline statistics for 1990. *The Connection, 9:* Spring, 1991.

Coyle, C., and Kinney, W.: A comparison of leisure and gambling motives of compulsive gamblers. *Therapeutic Recreation Journal, 24:* 32-39, 1990.

Cruz, Humberto: For many people, day trading no more than online gambling. *Milwaukee Journal Sentinel,* 2D, May 16, 1999.

Cunningham-Williams, Renee, Cottler, Linda B., Compton, Wilson M., Spitznagel, Edward L., and Ben-Abdallah, Arbi: Problem gambling and comorbid psychiatric and substance use disorders among drug users recruited from drug treatment and community settings. *Journal of Gambling Studies, 16:* 347-376, 2000.

Custer, Robert, and Milt, Harry: *When Luck Runs Out: Help for Compulsive Gamblers and Their Families.* New York: Facts on File Publications, 1985.

Fabozzi, Frank J., and Kipnis, Gregory M.: *The Handbook of Stock Index Futures and Options.* Homewood, IL: Dow Jones-Irwin, 1989.

Frank, Michael L., Lester, David, and Wexler, Arnold: Suicidal behavior among members of Gamblers Anonymous. *Journal of Gambling Studies,* 7:249-253, 1991.

Fredman, Catherine: Obsessive, compulsive and, so far, successful. *Fidelity Outlook,* 12-15, Summer, 1999.

Getty, Heather A., Watson, Jeanne, and Frisch, G. Ron: A comparison of depression and styles of coping in male and female GA members and controls. *Journal of Gambling Studies, 16:* 377-391, 2000.

Giacopassi, David, Stitt, B. Grant, and Vandiver, Margaret: An analysis of the relationship of alcohol to casino gambling among college students. *Journal of Gambling Studies, 14:*135-149, 1998.

Graham, John R., and Lowenfeld, Beverly H.: Personality dimensions of the pathological gambler. *Journal of Gambling Behavior, 2:*58-66, Summer, 1986.

Green, Marian.: All wired up, no place to go: America lags behind in the global internet gaming race. *International Gaming and Wagering Business, 20*:1 and 32-36, November, 1999.

Horodecki, Izabela: The treatment model of the guidance center for gamblers and their relatives in Vienna/Austria. *Journal of Gambling Studies, 8*:115-129, 1992.

Jacobs, Durand F.: A general theory of addictions: rationale for and evidence supporting a new approach for understanding and treating addictive behaviors. In Shaffer, Howard J., Stein, Sharon A., Gambino, Blase, and Cummings, Thomas N.(Eds.): *Compulsive Gambling: Theory, Research, and Practice*. Lexington, Lexington Books, 1989, pp. 35-64.

Jaffe, Charles A.: Crossing the line: Therapist says that for some, investing is no different than gambling. *The Boston Globe*, E1 & E3, December 15, 1999.

Jang, Ho-Chan, Lee, Bongkoo, Park, Minkyung, and Stokowski, Patricia A.: Measuring underlying meanings of gambling from the perspective of enduring involvement. *Journal of Travel Research, 38*:230-238, 2000.

Jesdanun, Anick: Internet gambling on the rise as Super Bowl nears. *The Tallahassee (FL) Democrat*, 1B, January 29, 2000.

Kruedelbach, N., Walker, H., and Rugle, L.: A Comparison of pathological gamblers in two residential treatment facilities. Paper presented at the 13th National Conference on Gambling Behavior, Detroit, June, 1999.

Ladoucuer, R., Dube, D., and Bujold, A.: Prevalence of pathological gambling and related problems among college students in the Quebec metropolitan area. *Canadian Journal of Psychiatry, 39*:289-293, 1994.

Lesieur, Henry R.: *The Chase: Career of the Compulsive Gambler*. Rochester, VT: Schenkman Books, 1984.

Lesieur, Henry R.: The female pathological gambler. In Eadington, W.R. (Ed.): *Gambling Research: Proceedings of the Seventh International Conference on Gambling and Risk Taking*. Reno, Bureau of Business and Economic Research, University of Nevada, Reno: 1988.

Lesieur, Henry R.: Testimony for expert panel on pathological gambling. National Gambling Impact Study Commission, Atlantic City, January 22, 1998a.

Lesieur, Henry R.: Costs and treatment of pathological gambling. *The Annals, 556*: 153-169, 1998b.

Lesieur, Henry R., Cross, J., Frank, M., Welch, M., and Mark, M.: Gambling and pathological gambling among university students. *Addictive Behaviors, 16*:517-527, 1991.

Lesieur, Henry R., Blume, Sheila B., and Zoppa, R.: Alcoholism, drug abuse, and gambling. *Alcoholism: Clinical and Experimental Research, 10*:33-38, 1986.

Lesieur, Henry R., and Blume, Sheila B.: Characteristics of pathological gamblers identified among patients on a psychiatric admission service. *Hospital and Community Psychiatry, 41*:1009-1012, 1990.

Lesieur, Henry R., and Blume, Sheila B.: When lady luck loses: Women and compulsive gambling. In Nan van den Bergh (ed.), *Feminist Perspectives on Addictions*. New York, Springer Publications, 181-197, 1991.

Lesieur, Henry R., and Heineman, M.: Pathological gambling among youthful multiple substance abusers in a therapeutic community. *British Journal of Addiction, 83*:765-761, 1988.

Lesieur, Henry R., and Marks, Marie: *Women Who Gamble Too Much.* Washington, DC: National Council on Problem Gambling, 1993.

Lesieur, Henry R., and Rosenthal, Richard J.: Pathological gambling: A review of the literature. *Journal of Gambling Studies, 7*:5-40, 1991.

McCormick, R. A., and Taber, J. I.: Attributional style in pathological gamblers in treatment. *Journal of Abnormal Psychology, 97*:368-370, 1988.

McCormick, R. A., Russo, A., Ramirez, L., and Taber, J.: Affective disorders among pathological gamblers seeking treatment. *American Journal of Psychiatry, 141*:215-218, 1984.

McCown, William G., and Keiser, R.: *Addiction, Fantasy, and Perception: The Role of Protective Techniques in Assessment and Treatment Planning of Addicted Individuals.* Mahwah, NJ: Erlbaum, 2000.

Merton, Robert K.: 1957. *Social Theory and Social Structure.* New York, Free Press.

Pasternak, Andrew V., and Fleming, Michael F.: Prevalence of gambling disorders in a primary care setting. *Archives of Family Medicine, 8*:515-520, 1999.

Pavalko, Ronald M.: Problem gambling: The hidden addiction. *National Forum, 79*:28-32, 1999.

Pavalko, Ronald M., and Teske, Carole A.: Gambling and the internet. Paper presented at the Second Annual Wisconsin Council on Problem Gambling Statewide Conference, Green Bay: March, 2000.

Quinn, Jane Bryant: *Making the Most of Your Money.* New York: Simon and Schuster, 1991.

Rosenthal, Richard J., and Rugle, Loreen: A psychodynamic approach to the treatment of pathological gambling: Part I. Achieving abstinence. *Journal of Gambling Studies, 10*:21-42, 1994.

Schauerte, M.: Legislator in Illinois wants to outlaw using internet to gamble. *St Louis Post-Dispatch,* C3, January 24, 1999.

Schneider, Sue: Growing pains online. *International Gaming and Wagering Business, 22*: 41, January, 2001.

Schwarz, Jurgen, and Lindner, Andreas: Inpatient treatment of male pathological gamblers in Germany. *Journal of Gambling Studies, 8*:93 107, 1992.

Smart, R.G., and Ferris, J.: Alcohol, drugs, and gambling in the Ontario adult population. *Canadian Journal of Psychiatry, 41*:36-45, 1996.

Steinberg, Marvin A., and Harris, Judah J.: Problem gambling in the stock market: An enormous problem ignored. Paper presented at Eighth National Conference on Gambling Behavior, Seattle, July, 1994.

Sullivan, S.: Why compulsive gamblers are a high suicide risk. *Community Mental Health in New Zealand, 8*:40-47, 1994.

Taber, Julian I., , Russo, Angel M., Adkins, Bonnie J., and McCormick, Richard A.: Ego strength and achievement motivation in pathological gamblers. *Journal of Gambling Behavior, 2*:69-80, 1996.

U.S. Bureau of the Census: *Statistical Abstract of the United States*, Washington: Government Printing Office, 103, Table 141, 1999.

Walker, Michael B.: Some problems with the concept of "gambling addiction": Should theories of addiction be generalized to include excessive gambling? *Journal of Gambling Behavior, 5*:179-200, 1989.

Chapter 3

ASSESSMENT AND DIAGNOSIS OF PROBLEM GAMBLING

There are four assessment instruments that can be used to diagnose problem gambling. These are the DSM IV Criteria, Gamblers Anonymous 20 Questions, the South Oaks Gambling Screen (SOGS), and the NORC DSM-IV Screen for Gambling Problems. In this chapter, the development of these tools and their use will be discussed.

THE DSM-IV CRITERIA

This instrument was introduced in Chapter 1 and used to develop an understanding of the basic nature of problem gambling in Chapter 2 (see Table 1.1). Strictly speaking, the DSM-IV Criteria identify "pathological" gambling and are designed to be used in a clinical setting. Diagnosis involves a clinician reaching a conclusion on the basis of information obtained directly from the client. When possible, clinicians may supplement information from the client with information from other sources such as friends and family members, other treatment professionals, etc. The criteria also can be thought of as a set of "symptoms" indicative of problem gambling. The clinician's task is to obtain as much information as possible about the client's gambling behavior and then determine whether that behavior "fits" the criteria. According to the American Psychiatric Association, if a person's behavior exhibits at least five of these criteria, he or she should be considered a "pathological gambler."

Several things about this assessment tool need to be noted. Clearly, the diagnosis of pathological gambling is based on the clinician's judgment. This raises the possibility that two or more clinicians looking at the same behavior may reach different conclusions, depending on how the client's behavior is interpreted.

In addition, different people may exhibit these criteria in varying degrees. For example, restlessness or irritability when attempting to cut down or stop gambling (criterion 4) may be mild in one person and extreme in another, or one person may have committed a single illegal act to get money with which to gamble, whereas another may have committed numerous such acts (criterion 8). Yet, if the criteria are applied in a mechanical way, both clients could be assessed the same way. In other words, this tool does not include a clear and explicit way of dealing with the degree to which a symptom of problem gambling is present.

Although five of these ten symptoms need to be exhibited before a diagnosis of "pathological gambling" is appropriate, a person exhibiting four, or even three, should not be dismissed as having no gambling problem at all. Similarly, the person who exhibits nine or ten symptoms probably has a much more serious problem with gambling than the person who exhibits five. Obviously, the diagnosis of pathological gambling is not a simple, mechanical yes/no decision, because symptoms will vary in the degree to which they are present.

Finally, the DSM-IV Criteria imply that each of the ten criteria are of equal importance in reaching the conclusion that a person is or is not a pathological gambler. This may or may not be the case, but the question has not been put to an empirical test. Some of these criteria may be more important or crucial than others. Among problem gambling counselors, there is a widely shared view that chasing one's losses (criterion 6) is a very important (if not the most important) indicator of problem gambling. Just how much more important it may be than the other criteria is uncertain. Although it would be useful to have these criteria rank ordered or weighted in importance, the information needed to do so simply is not available, creating the possibility that different clinicians may consciously or unconsciously "weight" these criteria differently.

GAMBLERS ANONYMOUS 20 QUESTIONS

As indicated in Chapter 1, Gamblers Anonymous (GA) has been in existence for more than forty years. GA's "treatment program" will be dealt with in Chapter 8. At this point, our interest is in an instrument developed by GA that can be used to assess people for problem gambling. Based on experience working with gamblers, GA has evolved a list of "20 Questions," which is presented in Table 3.1. If one were to go to a GA meeting seeking help for a gambling problem, one would be asked to complete this questionnaire to determine whether one had a gambling problem and, if so, how severe it was. According to GA, a problem gambler will answer "yes" to at least seven of these questions.

TABLE 3.1
GAMBLERS ANONYMOUS 20 QUESTIONS

1. Did you ever lose time from work or school due to gambling?

2. Has gambling ever made your home life unhappy?

3. Did gambling affect your reputation?

4. Have you ever felt remorse after gambling?

5. Did you ever gamble to get money with which to pay debts or otherwise solve financial difficulties?

6. Did gambling cause a decrease in your ambition or efficiency?

7. After losing did you feel you must return as soon as possible and win back your losses?

8. After a win did you have a strong urge to return and win more?

9. Did you often gamble until your last dollar was gone?

10. Did you ever borrow to finance your gambling?

11. Have you ever sold anything to finance gambling?

12. Were you reluctant to use "gambling money" for normal expenditures?

13. Did gambling make you careless of the welfare of yourself or your family?

14. Did you ever gamble longer than you had planned?

15. Have you ever gambled to escape worry or trouble?

16. Have you ever committed, or considered committing, an illegal act to finance gambling?

17. Did gambling cause you to have difficulty in sleeping?

18. Do arguments, disappointments, or frustrations create within you an urge to gamble?

19. Did you ever have an urge to celebrate any good fortune by a few hours of gambling?

20. Have you ever considered self destruction or suicide as a result of your gambling?

Source: Gamblers Anonymous, P.O. Box 17173, Los Angeles, CA 90017.
Reprinted by permission.

If these questions look similar to the DSM IV Criteria, it is no accident. In fact, GA's 20 Questions predate the DSM-IV Criteria. Psychiatrists and others who initially developed the DSM Criteria were familiar with GA, its program, and the 20 Questions. They borrowed liberally from the 20 Questions in developing the DSM Criteria (for an account of these early developments, see Castellani, 2000).

In using the 20 Questions to clinically assess a person for problem gambling, the instrument can be used in two ways. First, a person can be given the instrument and asked to answer yes or no to the questions. If this is done, it is important to follow up and discuss the questions with the person answering them to make sure that the questions were understood and also to clear up any ambiguities about the questions that the person may have. The instrument can also be used as an "interview schedule" in which a clinician asks the questions and records the responses. This latter method should be considered if there are any doubts about the client's ability to read or understand the questions. Use of an interview also gives the client the opportunity to ask about questions that may be unclear as the issues arise.

The same cautions raised about the DSM-IV Criteria apply to GA's 20 Questions. Conclusions about the existence of a gambling problem are based on the number of "yes" answers, but the intensity of those responses is not taken into account. Like the DSM-IV Criteria, the 20 Questions assume that each item is of equal importance for the purpose of scoring. Clearly, assessments using either the DSM-IV or GA 20 Questions need to be sensitive to these shortcomings and limitations in both instruments.

THE SOUTH OAKS GAMBLING SCREEN (SOGS)

The American Psychiatric Association included pathological gambling in its *Diagnostic and Statistical Manual* (DSM-III) for the first time in 1980. However, except for GA's 20 Questions, there did not exist any simple-to-use tools for screening for gambling problems. In the mid-1980s, a screening instrument was developed by Henry R. Lesieur, a sociologist, and Sheila B. Blume, a psychiatrist, at the South Oaks Institute of Alcoholism and Addictive Behavior Studies in Amityville, New York (Lesieur and Blume, 1987). It is loosely based on the DSM-III Criteria. The development of the SOGS included testing for reliability and validity on a number of groups, including hospital workers, university students, prison inmates, and inpatients in chemical dependence treatment programs. The instrument was revised in 1993 (Lesieur and Blume, 1993). A copy of the 1993 version of this instrument, along with the scoring sheet, is presented in Table 3.2.

TABLE 3.2
SOUTH OAKS GAMBLING SCREEN

Name _____ Date _____

1. Please indicate which of the following types of gambling you have done in your lifetime. For each type, mark one answer: "not at all," "less than once a week," or "once a week or more."

	not at all	less than once a week	once a week or more	
a.	___	___	___	play cards for money
b.	___	___	___	bet on horses, dogs, or other animals (at OTB, the track, or with a bookie)
c.	___	___	___	bet on sports (parlay cards, with a bookie, or at Jai Alai)
d.	___	___	___	played dice games (including craps, over and under, or other dice games) for money
e.	___	___	___	gambled in a casino (legal or otherwise)
f.	___	___	___	played the numbers or bet on lotteries
g.	___	___	___	played bingo for money
h.	___	___	___	played the stock, options, and/or commodities market
i.	___	___	___	played slot machines, poker machines, or other gambling machines
j.	___	___	___	bowled, shot pool, played golf, or some other game of skill for money
k.	___	___	___	pull tabs or "paper" games other than lotteries
m.	___	___	___	some form of gambling not listed above please specify_____

2. What is the largest amount of money you have ever gambled with   on any one day?

_____ never have gambled   _____ more than $100 up to $1,000
_____ $1 or less   _____ more than $1,000 up to $10,000
_____ more than $1 up   _____ more than $10,000
    to $10
_____ more than $10 up
    to $100

3. Check which of the following people in your life has (or had) a gambling problem.

_____ father _____ mother _____ brother or sister _____ grandparent
_____ my spouse/partner _____ my child(ren) _____ another relative
_____ a friend or someone else important in my life

4. When you gamble, how often do you go back another day to win back money you lost?

_____ never
_____ some of the time (less than half the time I lost)
_____ most of the time I lost
_____ every time I lost

5. Have you ever claimed to be winning money gambling but weren't really? If fact, you lost?

_____ never (or never gamble)
_____ yes, less than half the time I lost
_____ yes, most of the time

6. Do you feel you have ever had a problem with betting money or gambling ?

_____ no
_____ yes, in the past but not now
_____ yes

7. Did you ever gamble more than you intend to?   ____ yes ____ no

8. Have people criticized your betting or told you thatyou had a gambling problem,
   regardless of whether or not you thought it was true?   ____ yes ____ no

9. Have you ever felt guilty about the way you gamble or what happens when you gamble?
                                                                   ____ yes ____ no

10. Have you ever felt like you would like to stop betting money or gambling but didn't
    think you could?   ____ yes ____ no

11. Have you ever hidden betting slips, lottery tickets, gambling money, I.O.U.s, or other signs
    of betting or gambling from your spouse, children, or other important people in your life?
                                                                   ____ yes ____ no

12. Have you ever argued with people you live with over how you handle money?
                                                                   ____ yes ____ no

13. (If you answered yes to question 12): Have money arguments ever centered on your
    gambling?   ____ yes ____ no

14. Have you ever borrowed from someone and not paid them back as a result of your
    gambling?   ____ yes ____ no

15. Have you ever lost time from work (or school) due to betting money or gambling?

_____ yes _____ no

16. If you borrowed money to gamble or to pay gambling debts, who   or where did you borrow from? (check "yes" or "no" for each)

	no	yes
a. from household money	( )	( )
b. from your spouse	( )	( )
c. from other relatives or in-laws	( )	( )
d. from banks, loan companies, or credit unions	( )	( )
e. from credit cards	( )	( )
f. from loan sharks	( )	( )
g. you cashed in stocks, bonds, or other securities	( )	( )
h. you sold personal of family property	( )	( )
i. you borrowed on your checking account (passed bad checks)	( )	( )
j. you have (had) a credit line with a bookie	( )	( )
k. you have (had) a credit line with a casino	( )	( )

South Oaks Gambling Screen Score Sheet

Scores on the SOGS itself are determined by adding up the number of questions which show an "at risk" response:

Questions 1, 2, and 3 not counted.

Question 4—most of the time I lose
or
every time I lose

Question 5—yes, less than half the time I lose
or
yes, most of the time

Question 6—yes, in the past but not now
or
yes

Question 7—yes
" 8—yes
" 9—yes
" 10—yes
" 11—yes
" 12 not counted
" 13—yes
" 14—yes
" 15—yes
" 16a—yes

" b–yes
" c–yes
" d–yes
" e–yes
" f–yes
" g–yes
" h–yes
" i–yes

* questions 16 j and k not counted

Total _____ (there are 20 questions which are counted)

0 = no problem

1-4 = some problem

5 or more = probable pathological gambler

Source: Lesieur, Henry R. and Blume, Sheila B.: 1993. Revising the South Oaks Gambling Screen in different settings. *Journal of Gambling Studies, 9*:213-219, 1993. ©South Oaks Foundation. Reprinted by Permission.

From its inception to 1999, the *South Oaks Gambling Screen* (SOGS) was the most widely used instrument for identifying problem gamblers. It was rapidly and widely adopted by counselors to screen for gambling problems in clinical settings. It also became the standard tool for identifying problem gamblers in "epidemiological" research where, using survey research techniques, the prevalence of problem gambling in a large population is estimated. By 1998, it had been used in more than 45 prevalence studies in the United States, Canada, Asia, and Europe (Shaffer et al., 1997).

As we will see later, a newer instrument (the NORC DSM-IV) has been developed and may become as extensively used, if not more so. Nevertheless, the SOGS remains a useful instrument for the clinical diagnosis of problem gambling.

The SOGS can be self-administered, or the questions can be asked of the subject by an interviewer. As with GA's 20 Questions, self-administered answers should be gone over with the person answering the questions to make sure that they were understood and to clarify any questions or responses that may be ambiguous or unclear.

The SOGS poses some of the same difficulties as the DSM IV Criteria and GA's 20 Questions and should be used with the same cautions. Because the questions are not "weighted," the implication is that each scored question measures behavior that is equal in importance to all other scored questions. This may or may not be the case.

Not all questions on the SOGS are scored (questions 1-3, 12, and 16 j and k are not scored). Questions 1-3 and 16 j and k provide general information about the extent and variety of a person's involvement with gambling. Question 12 sets the stage for question 13, which is scored. The maximum possible score on the SOGS is 20.

The interpretation of the scores is as follows:

5 or higher: probable pathological (compulsive) gambler

1-4: problem gambler (the person has a gambling problem but does not have sufficient symptoms to be considered a compulsive gambler)

This interpretation scheme is an improvement over the "yes/no" interpretation of the DSM IV and GA's 20 Questions because it explicitly acknowledges the existence of *degrees* of a gambling problem. The questions on the SOGS are typically asked on a "lifetime" basis but can also be asked for shorter time periods (e.g., past year, past six months).

Clearly, the questions on the SOGS reflect the DSM Criteria and are similar in many ways to GA's 20 questions. Studies that have assessed people using two or three of these instruments report very high correlations between them.

CASE STUDIES

Case studies are a useful way of illustrating the assessment process. Presented following are two case studies of assessments done by the author. They illustrate some of the difficulties and problems encountered in doing assessments. In both cases, the names of the people assessed are fictitious, and some of the details of the crimes they committed have been changed in the interest of protecting privacy. Both assessments were conducted before the availability of the NODS DSM IV Screen discussed later.

CASE STUDY ONE

Joey Findley: Dealing Drugs to Solve a Money Problem

I met Joey Findley in the offices of his lawyer in Milwaukee, Wisconsin, in the spring of 1993. His lawyer had called to ask if I would do an assessment of Joey for problem gambling. Joey had been arrested and plead guilty to drug-selling charges. He was coming up for sentencing soon, and based on what his lawyer had learned about Joey, it seemed that he had a gambling problem that might account for his involvement with drugs. Joey had no prior criminal record. Basically, the lawyer was looking for something that might persuade the judge to go easy on the sentence. Because Joey had already pleaded guilty to federal drug charges, he was looking at mandatory prison time, but the judge had some leeway in the severity of his sentence.

My evaluation took a little over three hours. We talked about his work career and personal life, as well as his gambling activities. I administered the South Oaks Gambling Screen (SOGS) and GA's 20 Questions.

At the time I evaluated him, Joey was 33 years old. He grew up on a farm in Wisconsin, the youngest of three children. Since graduating from high school he worked at a number of different jobs including construction labor, truck driving, and as a telemarketer.

Joey had never been married. At the time of his arrest he was living with a young woman with whom he had a relationship for the past five years.

About a year before his arrest, Joey had run out of ways to get money to gamble with and pay off his debts. He had borrowed from his parents, his girlfriend, a brother, and coworkers. He had about $35,000 in credit card debt, no job, and his car was about to be repossessed. Most importantly, he owed his bookie $15,000, and the bookie was getting very impatient. By accident, Joey ran into an old high school buddy, told him of his money problems, and asked him for a $15,000 loan. His friend said, "I'll do better than that. I'll give you the money up front, if you come and work for me." Joey agreed. The job involved transporting marijuana and cocaine from southern California to Wisconsin. Joey took care of the bookie, had a solid income, and was "back in action." Unfortunately, his travels (by car) from Wisconsin to California and back took him through Las Vegas, where his gambling losses took virtually all the money he was making.

What about Joey's gambling career? He had been a gambler since high school, betting mainly on football games and pool. After high school, his gambling expanded to just about every known form of legal and illegal gambling. His preference was for sports betting (professional and college football, basketball, baseball, and hockey). This of course got him involved with bookies. He indicated that during the 1992 football season his losses were around $25,000. He also bet on horse and dog races, and when he did, he would typically bet the "exotic" wagers–trifectas, perfectas, and daily doubles.

Joey was also an avid casino gambler. His favorite games were blackjack and craps. With the advent of Indian reservation and riverboat casinos in the early 1990s, getting to casino action was easier, although he made frequent trips to Nevada and occasionally to Atlantic City. He played slot machines and bought lottery tickets only occasionally. He had a preference for the table games, because they were "exciting." When playing craps, he would never count his money to see how he was doing. The only thing relevant was to keep making the bets. He especially liked the shouting and cheering that occurred at the craps tables when a player was "on a roll." When playing blackjack, he would move to another table when the dealer had to shuffle the cards, so that he would not miss any action. By far his favorite game was baccarat. He enjoyed sitting at the table with "high rollers" and betting $10,000 to $15,000 per hand. However, his bankroll was not sufficient to sustain this kind of action for very long.

Getting Joey to identify his biggest wins and losses and his best and worst gambling days was difficult. When I asked him how much money he thought he had lost during his whole gambling career, he said, "About $80,000." Then he quickly added, "But it could be $50,000 to $100,000 more." Like many problem gamblers, the amount he was wining and losing was irrelevant. Staying in action was all that mattered. Money became relevant only when he didn't have any or couldn't get any to gamble with.

During my assessment of Joey, he did something that I have seen a few other problem gamblers do, but he did it in an extreme way. When we first started talking, Joey was quite subdued, almost meek. But as he talked more about his gambling, he became increasingly animated, began pacing around the room, became louder, and started chain-smoking. It was as if just talking about his gambling sent him back into action. He seemed able to experience a "high" by reliving his past gambling experiences.

As far as the formal assessment results are concerned, Joey was clearly a problem gambler. He answered "yes" to 18 of GA's 20 questions. He was not quite sure about question 2 ("Has gambling ever made your home life unhappy?" because he was not married) and emphatically said "no" to question 20 ("Have you ever considered self-destruction or suicide as a result of your gambling?"). On the SOGS his "lifetime" score was 13, and for the six months before to his arrest his score was 12. On the DSM Criteria, it was my judgment that he met six of them.

What kind of insight did Joey have into his gambling behavior? He knew that his gambling was responsible for his current legal problems, his girlfriend's departure, and the utter confusion of his parents and siblings about what he had done. He has never seriously tried to cut back on his gambling or quit, although he did attend one GA meeting, which he found to be "silly." Gambling was so central a part of his life that it was difficult for him to think of any other way of living. I asked Joey what he would do if he had $5,000 right now. His first response was that he would head for the nearest casino. Then he quickly added that realistically he would give $2,000 to his parents (he had borrowed more than $10,000 from them over the years) and he would spend the rest gambling.

I appeared at the sentencing as an expert witness and presented the court with the results of my evaluation, including some of the details of Joey's gambling behavior described here. The judge seemed sympathetic but indicated that, for federal drug charges, prison time was mandatory. Joey got seven years in a federal prison. After the sentencing, I asked Joey's lawyer what effect, if any, my testimony had on the sentence. His response was "You probably saved him two years." (*Source:* From the author's files.)

CASE STUDY TWO

Carl Holtsman: Resorting to Forgery to Get Gambling Money

I assessed Carl at the request of a Public Defender in a central Wisconsin county. I interviewed him in the county jail where he was being held pending trial. He was charged with seven counts of forgery. He had cashed checks on the account of his friend and roommate at various Wisconsin and Minnesota casinos, when he ran out of gambling money. He stressed that he had just "borrowed" the money and fully intended to pay it back as soon as he had a few good (gambling) wins and was back on his feet financially. There was also a pending charge of theft by virtue of failing to return a rented vehicle, which he was using to travel around to different casinos.

At the time I did my assessment, Carl was 22 years old. A high school graduate, his employment before his arrest included unskilled construction work, sales, telemarketing, and golf course maintenance. Although he had no juvenile criminal record, he had been arrested at age 18 for fourth-degree sexual assault and served nine months in a Wisconsin county jail.

Gambling had been an interest of Carl's for as far back as he could remember. Shooting baskets for money with friends at the age of nine was his earliest recollection of gambling. He also bet with friends on pool and golf, games he learned to play in early adolescence. In high school, he frequently bet on sporting events, mainly high school, college, and professional football games.

Carl celebrated his eighteenth birthday with a trip to a Wisconsin Native American casino and "fell in love" with blackjack. From then until his arrest for forgery, life involved working just enough to get money for food and a place to sleep and gambling. His gambling interests expanded to include craps and roulette (which he went to Las Vegas to play). To a lesser extent he also played slots and video poker and bought an occasional lottery ticket.

Losing track of time while gambling was something that Carl experienced frequently. Increased heartbeat, sweaty palms, and stomach cramps were also reported as were severe headaches and sleeplessness after heavy losses. On one occasion, he played blackjack for four days straight (with no sleep) at a Wisconsin casino.

At different times during his (comparatively short) gambling career, Carl borrowed money from friends, his girlfriend, and his grandmother. At the worst point, he owed about $8,000. He also indicated that he "borrowed (i.e., stole) $400 from a store in which he was working. For at least two years, he returned Christmas presents for cash, which he then used to gamble with. He also got a $1,500 loan from a bank using his car (a high school graduation present) as collateral.

Like many problem gamblers, Carl had some difficulty recalling his biggest wins and losses. He recalled a day in Las Vegas when he won $4,000 playing roulette and a $12,000 loss at blackjack over a day and a half period seems to be his biggest loss.

In terms of the formal assessment results, Carl clearly met six of the DSM criteria. On Gamblers Anonymous 20 Questions, he answered yes to 18 of them, and he scored 17 on the SOGS.

Interestingly, Carl recognizes that he has a serious gambling problem. He has gone to Gamblers Anonymous meetings several times but has not really become involved in the program. He also had himself banned from one Wisconsin Native American casino, although he managed to get in and gamble there after being "self-excluded."

I appeared as an expert witness at Carl's trial. Neither the judge nor the prosecuting attorney seemed very interested in his gambling problem. He was sentenced to three years in a state prison. I learned later that he was paroled after serving a little more than a year and was getting treatment from a qualified problem gambling counselor.

(*Source*: From the author's files.)

THE NORC DSM-IV SCREEN FOR GAMBLING PROBLEMS (NODS)

There is a complex story behind the development of our last screening instrument, the NORC DSM-IV Screen for Gambling Problems (NODS). It includes technical questions and problems raised about the SOGS, as well as a mandate from a federal commission created to study the impact of gambling.

No tool or test for physical or psychological problems is 100 percent perfect. They all produce errors of two kinds. When a test incorrectly diagnoses a person as having a problem that does not exist, this is called a *false positive*. Conversely, a person may have a problem but may be diagnosed as not having it; this is called a *false negative*.

In studies done in the early 1990s, several "misclassification" issues were raised about the SOGS. When a psychological screen is used in a clinical setting where the prevalence of the problem can safely be assumed to be high, the screen works well. However, in a large, non-clinical population where prevalence is low, accuracy of the screen declines (Dohrenwend, 1995).

A study done in the early 1990s in New Zealand identified these kinds of errors in the SOGS when it is used to identify the prevalence of gambling problems in the general population. In addition to a general population survey, face-to-face interviews were conducted with "true" pathological gamblers and subgroups of nonproblem gamblers, lifetime problem gamblers, and lifetime probable pathological gamblers. The study concluded that the SOGS asked on a *lifetime* basis did a good job of detecting current pathological gamblers. However, while doing a good job of identifying pathological gamblers, the lifetime SOGS had a high rate of false positives. Asked on a *current* basis, the SOGS produced fewer false positives but had a higher rate of false negatives. Another way of putting this is that the lifetime SOGS overestimated the level of pathological gambling, but the current SOGS underestimated it (Abbott and Volberg, 1996). Just how people interpret the questions on the SOGS is another issue that has raised concerns about the use of this instrument (Ladouceur et al., 2000).

Concerns have also been raised about the relevance of some of the questions in the SOGS for the "new" gamblers created by the expansion of legal gambling in the late 1980s and 1990s. Questions dealing with borrowing from loan sharks, having a credit line with a bookie, or cashing in stocks and bonds were more relevant to middle-class male gamblers of the 1970s and early 1980s than they are to the increasing number of young adults and middle-age women participating in gambling more recently (National Opinion Research Center et al., 1999).

The final stimulus for a new screening instrument came from the National Gambling Impact Study Commission (NGISC). Created by Congress in 1996, its task was to study and report on the economic and social impacts of gambling in the United States. One of the things the Commission wanted to know about was the prevalence of pathological and problem gambling. The NGISC required that the DSM-IV Criteria be used to identify the level of problem and pathological gambling. Because the SOGS was loosely based on an older set of DSM criteria, a new measure had to be developed. The NGISC contracted with the National Opinion Research Center (NORC) at the

University of Chicago to perform this task. NORC assembled a research team that developed the "NORC DSM-IV Screen for Gambling Problems" (acronymed the NODS).

TABLE 3.3
THE NORC DSM IV SCREEN (NODS)

The screen is set up to run first a lifetime screen for all items and then ask about the past year only for those items endorsed for lifetime.

SCORING:

Lifetime: Add one point for every YES to any of the following items: 1 or 2, 3, 5, 7, 8 or 9, 10, 12, 13, 14 or 15 or 16, 17

Past year: Add one point for every YES to any of the following items: 18 or 19, 20, 22, 24, 25 or 26, 27, 29, 30, 31 or 32 or 33, 34

If gambler responds YES to more than one item in a response cluster (e.g., 8 or 9), count them together as a single point.

INTERPRETATION OF SCORES:

0 = low-risk gambler
1 or 2 = at risk gambler
3 or 4 = problem gambler
5 or more = pathological gambler (by DSM Criteria)

LIFETIME PROBLEMS

1. Have there ever been periods lasting two weeks or longer when you spent a lot of time thinking about your gambling experiences or planning out future gambling ventures or bets?

   YES NO

2. Have there ever been periods lasting two weeks or longer when you spent a lot of time thinking about ways of getting money to gamble with?

   YES NO

3. Have there ever been periods when you needed to gamble with increasing amounts of money or with larger bets than before in order to get the same feeling of excitement?

   YES NO

4. Have you ever tried to stop, cut down, or control your gambling?

   YES (GO TO 5) NO (GO TO 8)

5. On one or more of the times when you tried to stop, cut down, or control your gambling, were you restless or irritable?

YES NO

6. Have you tried *but not succeeded* in stopping, cutting down, or controlling your gambling?

YES (GO TO 7) NO (GO TO 8)

7. Has this happened three or more times?

YES NO

8. Have you ever gambled as a way to escape from personal problems?

YES NO

9. Have you ever gambled to relieve uncomfortable feelings such as guilt, anxiety, helplessness, or depression?

YES NO

10. Has there ever been a period when, if you lost money gambling one day, you would return another day to get even?

YES NO

11. Have you ever lied to family members, friends, or others about how much you gamble or how much money you lost on gambling?

YES (GO TO 12) NO (GO TO 13)

12. Has this happened three or more times?

YES NO

13. Have you ever written a bad check or taken something that didn't belong to you from family members or anyone else to pay for your gambling?

YES NO

14. Has your gambling ever caused serious or repeated problems in your relationships with any of your family members or friends?

YES NO .

15. ANSWER ONLY IF YOU ARE IN SCHOOL. Has your gambling caused you any problems in school, such as missing classes or days of school or your grades dropping?

YES NO

16. Has your gambling ever caused you to lose a job, have trouble with your job, or miss out on an important job or career opportunity?

YES NO

17. Have you ever needed to ask family members or anyone else to loan you money or otherwise bail you out of a desperate money situation that was largely caused by your gambling?

YES NO

PAST-YEAR PROBLEMS

COMPLETE THIS SECTION ONLY IF YOU HAVE GAMBLED IN THE PAST YEAR.

18. (ANSWER ONLY IF 1 = YES)
Since (current month) (last year), have there been any periods lasting two weeks or longer when you spent a lot of time thinking about your gambling experiences or planning future gambling ventures or bets?

YES NO

19. (ANSWER ONLY IF 2 = YES)
Since (current month) (last year), have there been periods lasting two weeks or longer when you spent a lot of time thinking about ways of getting money to gamble with?

YES NO

20. (ANSWER ONLY IF 3 = YES)
Since (current month) (last year), have there been periods when you needed to gamble with increasing amounts of money or with larger bets than before in order to get the same feeling of excitement?

YES NO

21. (ANSWER ONLY IF 4 = YES)
Since (current month) (last year), have you tried to stop, cut down, or control your gambling?

YES (GO TO 22) NO (GO TO 25)

22. (ANSWER ONLY IF 5 = YES)
Since (current month) (last year), on one or more of the times when you tried to stop, cut down, or control your gambling, were you restless or irritable?

YES NO

23. (ANSWER ONLY IF 6 = YES)
    Since (current month) (last year), have you tried but not succeeded in stopping, cutting down, or controlling your gambling?

    YES NO

24. (ANSWER ONLY IF 7 = YES)
    Since [current month) [last year), has this happened three or more times?

    YES NO

25. (ANSWER ONLY IF 8 = YES)
    Since (current month) (last year), have you gambled as a way to escape from personal problems?

    YES NO

26. (ANSWER ONLY IF 9 = YES)
    Since (current month) (last year), have you gambled to relieve uncomfortable feelings such as guilt, helplessness, or depression?

    YES NO

27. (ANSWER ONLY IF 10 = YES)
    Since (current month) (last year), has there ever been a period   when, if you lost money gambling on one day, you would often return another day to get even?

    YES NO

28. (ANSWER ONLY IF 11 = YES)
    Since (current month) (last year), have you more than once lied to family members, friends, or others about how much you gamble or how much money you lost on gambling?

    YES (GO TO 29) NO (GO TO 30)

29. (ANSWER ONLY IF 12 = YES)
    Has this happened three or more times?

    YES NO

30. (ANSWER ONLY IF 13 = YES)
    Since (current month) (last year), have you written a bad check or taken money that didn't belong to you from family members or anyone else in order to pay for your gambling?

    YES NO

31. (ANSWER ONLY IF 14 = YES)
    Since (current month) (last year), has your gambling caused serious or repeated problems in your relationships with any family members or friends?

    YES NO

32. (ANSWER ONLY IF 15 = YES)
    Since (current month) (last year), has your gambling caused you any problems in school, such as missing classes or days of school or getting worse grades?

    YES NO

33. (ANSWER ONLY IF 16 = YES)
    Since (current month) (last year), has your gambling caused you to lose a job, have trouble with your job, or miss out on an important job or career opportunity?

    YES NO

34. (ANSWER ONLY IF 17 = YES)
    Since (current month) (last year), have you needed to ask family members or anyone else to loan you money or otherwise bail you out of a desperate money situation that was largely caused by your gambling?

    YES NO

Source: National Opinion Research Center at the University of Chicago, Gemini Research, The Lewin Group, and Christiansen, Cummings, and Associates: *Gambling Impact and Behavior Study: Report to the National Gambling Impact Study Commission*, April 1, 1999, www.norc.uchicago.edu (downloaded April 20, 1999).

The NODS is reproduced in Table 3.3. The instrument measures preoccupation with gambling, tolerance, withdrawal, loss of control, use of gambling to escape from problems, chasing losses, lying, committing illegal acts, risking significant relationships, and bailouts. Table 3.4 shows how the questions in the NODS align with the DSM-IV criteria. Compared to the SOGS, the NODS is more restrictive and demanding. For example, a respondents must indicate that they have lied about their gambling three or more times before this question is scored.

TABLE 3.4
DSM-IV CRITERIA AND CORRESPONDING NODS LIFETIME QUESTION

DSM-IV Criteria	NODS Question(s)
Preoccupation	1 and 2
Tolerance	3
Withdrawal	4 and 5
Loss of control	6 and 7
Escape	8 and 9
Chasing	10
Lying	11 and 12
Illegal acts	13
Risked significant relationship	14, 15, and 16
Bailout	17

Source: National Opinion Research Center at the University of Chicago, Gemini Research, The Lewin Group, and Christiansen, Cummings, and Associates: *Gambling Impact and Behavior Study: Report to the National Gambling Impact Study Commission*, April 1, 1999, www.norc.uchicago.edu (downloaded April 20, 1999). Chapter 2, p. 18.

Using responses to the NODS, four different kinds of gamblers and three levels of gambling problems are used. They are:

Low-Risk Gambler	Never gambled or, if gambled, never lost more than $100 in a single day or year, *or*, lost more than $100 in a single day or year but reported no DSM-IV Criteria.
	Lost more than $100 in a single day or year *and* reported:
At-Risk Gambler	One or two DSM-IV Criteria

Problem Gambler   Three or four DSM-IV Criteria

Pathological Gambler   Five or More DSM-IV Criteria

In all likelihood, the NODS will replace the SOGS in survey research that seeks to estimate problem gambling prevalence rates in large populations (a topic discussed more fully in Chapter 4). The NODS is so new that it is uncertain whether it will replace the SOGS for use in clinical settings. One of its positive features is that it identifies degrees of a gambling problem more precisely than the other instruments. It distinguishes between low-risk gamblers, at-risk gamblers, problem gamblers, and pathological gamblers (see the "Interpretation of Scores" section of the instrument in Table 3.3).

SUMMARY

Four tools are used to diagnose problem gambling: the DSM IV Criteria, Gamblers Anonymous 20 Questions, the South Oaks Gambling Screen (SOGS), and the NORC DSM-IV Screen for Gambling Problems (NODS). Although all these instruments have a cutoff point for deciding whether a person is a problem gambler, they need to be used judiciously. Those scoring just below the cutoff may still have a gambling problem, and those scoring just above the cutoff may be quite different than those scoring at the top of the scale. It is important that diagnoses do more than just conclude that a person is or is not a problem gambler; they need to determine the degree to which a gambling problem is present or absent.

REFERENCES

Abbott, Max W., and Volberg, Rachel A.: The New Zealand national survey of problem and pathological gambling. *Journal of Gambling Studies, 12*:143-160, 1996.

Castellani, Brian: *Pathological Gambling: The Making of a Medical Problem.* Albany: State University of New York Press, 2000.

Dohrenwend B. P.: The problem of validity in field studies of psychological disorders, revisited. In Ming, T., Tsuang, Tohen, Mauricio, and Zahner, Gwendolyn E.P. (Eds.): *Textbook in Psychiatric Epidemiology*, New York: Wiley-Liss, 1995.

Ladouceur, Robert, Bouchard, Carole, Rheaume, Nadis, Jacques, Christian, Ferland, Francine, Leblond, Jean, and Walker, Michael: Is the SOGS an accurate measure of pathological gambling among children, adolescents, and adults? *Journal of Gambling Studies, 16*:1-24, 2000.

Lesieur, Henry R., and Blume, Sheila B.: The South Oaks Gambling Screen (SOGS): A new instrument for the identification of pathological gamblers. *American Journal of Psychiatry, 144*:1184-1188, 1987.

Lesieur, Henry R., and Blume, Sheila B.: Revising the South Oaks Gambling Screen in different settings. *Journal of Gambling Studies, 9*:213-219, 1993.

National Opinion Research Center, Gemini Research, The Lewin Group, and Christiansen/Cummings Associates: *Gambling Impact and Behavior Study: Report to the National Gambling Impact Study Commission.* www.norc.uchicago.edu, downloaded April 1, 1999.

Shaffer, Howard J., Hall, Matthew N., and Vander Bilt, Joni: *Estimating the Prevalence of Disordered Gambling Behavior in the United States and Canada" A Meta-Analysis.* Cambridge, MA: Harvard Medical School, December 15, 1997.

Chapter 4

THE PREVALENCE OF PROBLEM GAMBLING

Just how prevalent is problem gambling? How is the prevalence of problem gambling related to such demographic variables as age, gender, economic status, marital status, race, and ethnicity? How is problem gambling related to other disorders? Has problem gambling increased over time? Has the growth of legal commercial gambling led to an increase in problem gambling? These are important questions. They bear on a number of issues, including the need for problem gambling counselors, the need for treatment programs, and the question of who is "at risk" for developing gambling related problems.

NATIONAL SURVEYS

Two national studies have attempted to estimate how prevalent problem gambling is in the general population. Both were conducted under the auspices of congressionally mandated "Commissions" charged with assessing, among other things, the prevalence of problem gambling.

The first study was conducted in 1975 by the University of Michigan's Institute for Social Research for the National Commission on the Review of National Policy Toward Gambling. The study found that 0.77 percent of the American adult population (approximately 1.1 million people at that time) could be considered "probable compulsive gamblers" (Kallick et al. 1979).

The second was carried out in 1998 by the National Opinion Research Center (NORC) of the University of Chicago for the National Gambling Impact Study Commission (NGISC) created by the U.S. Congress in 1996. The NORC study is based on telephone interviews with a random sample of 2,417 adults and face-to-face interviews with 530 patrons at a variety of gambling facilities. The study concluded that 1.2 percent of the adult population (about 2.5 million people) were "pathological gamblers;" (i.e., they met at least five of the DSM-IV criteria). An additional 1.5 percent (about 3 million people) were "problem gamblers," who met three or four of the DSM-IV criteria. Another 7.7 percent (a little more than 15 million people) who met one or two of the DSM-IV criteria were classified as being "at risk" of becoming problem gamblers (National Opinion Research Center et al., 1999).

Comparing these two studies indicates an increase in the prevalence of problem gambling. However, they are not strictly comparable, because different instruments were used to identify the presence of a gambling problem.

STATE SURVEYS

Since the mid-1980s, a number of state surveys have been conducted, usually at the initiative of state lottery boards and gaming commissions. These surveys are sufficient in number and have been done in such a variety of states and regions that they provide an supplemental way of estimating and describing the prevalence of problem gambling throughout the country, as well as permitting regional comparisons. In a few states "replications" have been done, making it possible to look at changes in the prevalence of problem gambling over time. These surveys were done before the development of the NODS and rely on the SOGS as the measure of pathological and problem gambling.

Table 4.1 presents a summary overview of this research, with survey results grouped by region. In most surveys, a distinction is made between "probable pathological gamblers" (those who score 5 or higher on the South Oaks Gambling Screen) and "problem gamblers" (those who score 3 or 4 on the SOGS). In Table 4.1 and the discussion that follows, these two groups are combined and will be referred to as "problem gamblers." Some surveys also make a distinction on the basis of peoples' response to the SOGS questions for different time frames such as "lifetime," "the past year," or "the past six months." In Table 4.1, all prevalence rates are for lifetime responses on the SOGS.

TABLE 4.1
LIFETIME PREVALENCE RATES FOR PROBLEM GAMBLING

Region and State	Year	Sample Size	Prevalence Rate (%)
Northeast			
New York	1986	1,000	4.2
New York	1996	1,829	7.3
New Jersey	1988	1,000	4.2
Maryland	1988	750	3.9
Massachusetts	1989	750	4.4
Connecticut	1991	1,000	6.3
Midwest/Central			
Iowa	1989	750	1.7
Iowa	1995	1,500	5.4
Michigan	1997	3,942	5.4
Michigan	1999	1,717	4.9
Minnesota	1990	1,251	2.4
Minnesota	1994	1,028	4.4
South Dakota	1991	1,560	2.8
South Dakota	1993	1,767	2.3
Montana	1992	1,020	3.6
North Dakota	1992	1,517	3.5
West			
California	1990	1,250	4.1
Texas	1992	6,308	4.8
Texas	1995	7,015	5.4
Washington State	1992	1,502	5.1
South			
Georgia	1994	1,551	4.4
Louisiana	1995	1,818	7.0
Louisiana	1998	1,800	5.8
Mississippi	1996	1,014	6.8

Sources: Cox, Sue, Lesieur, Henry R., Rosenthal, Richard J., and Volberg, Rachel A.: *Problem and Pathological Gambling in America: The National Picture*, Columbia, MD: National Council on Problem Gambling, 1997; Emerson, Michael O., and Laundergan, J. Clark,: Gambling and problem gambling among adult Minnesotans: Changes 1990 to 1994. *Journal of Gambling Studies, 12*:291-304, 1996; Gullickson, Arlen, Hartmann, David J., and Wiersma, William: *A Survey of GamblingBehaviors in Michigan, 1999*, Ann Arbor, Michigan Department of Community Health, 1999; Ryan, Timothy P., and Speyrer, Janet F., *Gambling in Louisiana, A Benefit/Cost Analysis*, Shreveport, LA, Louisiana State University Medical Center, April, 1999; Volberg, Rachel A., *Gambling and Problem Gambling in Iowa: A Replication Study*, Roaring Springs, PA: Gemini Research, July, 1995; Volberg, Rachel A.: Prevalence studies of problem gambling in the United States. *Journal of Gambling Studies, 12*:111-128, 1996; and Wallisch, Lynn S.: *Gambling in Texas: 1995 Surveys of Adult and Adolescent Gambling Behavior*, Austin, Texas Commission on Alcohol and Drug Abuse, August, 1996.

If we take an average of these prevalence rates, it seems that about 4.3 percent of the adult population are problem gamblers. In 1995 there were just less than 187 million people in the United States age 20 and older (U.S. Bureau of the Census, 1996). If the rate of problem gambling is 4.3 percent, that translates into a little more than 8 million problem gamblers.

Several important patterns are in the data in Table 4.1. Prevalence rates tend to cluster into two groups. In the Midwest/Central region, with *comparatively* little gambling, prevalence rates tend to be lower than in the other regions. For example, in 1989 Iowa had a very low prevalence rate. This survey was done two years before riverboat casinos began operating. The other regions (Northeast/West/South) have higher prevalence rates. Especially noteworthy is Connecticut, with substantial accessibility to gambling (Foxwoods, the largest Indian reservation casino in the country) and Atlantic City), and Louisiana and Mississippi, where riverboat and waterborne casinos have become widespread in recent years.

Another pattern involves changes over time in the prevalence rate of particular states. As the data in Table 4.1 indicate, there are seven states in which "replication" studies have been done (New York, Iowa, Michigan, Minnesota, South Dakota, Texas, and Louisiana). The results of these replications are somewhat mixed, but they do contain a pattern. The largest increase in the prevalence of problem gambling occurred in New York and Iowa. During the time period covered, Iowa experienced a very substantial increase in the availability of legal (mainly riverboat casino) gambling. Between the first and second New York study, the Mashantucket Pequot's Native American casino "Foxwoods" came on line in Connecticut, and Atlantic City casinos increased in number, size, and their marketing efforts. The time period between the original baseline and replication studies was also longer for these two states than the other four, providing greater opportunity for increases in problem gambling to emerge (10 years for New York and 6 years for Iowa).

Minnesota experienced the next highest increase in the prevalence of problem gambling (2.0 percent). In Texas the increase was very small (0.6 percent). In Michigan and South Dakota the prevalence of problem gambling actually decreased by 0.5 percent. In Texas and South Dakota only three years elapsed between the baseline and replication studies, and in Michigan the time between surveys was only two years. Given the short time periods between surveys in these states, one would not expect to see significant changes. Louisiana's prevalence rate also dropped the most over the three years that elapsed between the first and second surveys.

Although there are exceptions, these patterns provide qualified support for the generalization that the more available and accessible gambling is, the higher the prevalence of problem gambling.

SECTOR-SPECIFIC STUDIES

One intriguing question that recurs in the study of problem gambling is whether some forms of gambling are more likely to produce problem gambling than others. At this point we cannot say with precision that, for example, blackjack players are "x" times more likely than bingo players to become problem gamblers, or that video poker is "x" times as addictive as craps. This whole issue becomes even more complicated by the fact that most gamblers engage, over time, in more than one kind of gambling activity.

However, there is some research that has focused on the prevalence of problem gambling in different gambling venues. The 1998 NORC survey discussed earlier included interviews with 530 patrons at different gambling facilities. These included patrons at Nevada, Atlantic City, riverboat, and Native American casinos (53 percent), lottery ticket purchasers (36 percent), and patrons at race tracks (11 percent). The people interviewed at these gambling venues had much higher rates of pathological, problem, and at-risk gambling than was found in the general population survey. For example, 7.9 percent of the patrons at these venues were classified as *lifetime pathological* gamblers compared with to only 0.8 percent in the general population; 5.3 percent of the patrons were classified as *lifetime problem* gamblers compared with 1.3 percent in the general population; and 17.9 percent of the patrons were judged to be *lifetime at-risk* gamblers compared with 7.9 percent of the general population (National Opinion Research Center et al., 1999).

A very unique study of the prevalence of problem gambling among casino patrons was done in Great Britain in 1995. Interviews were conducted with 1,105 casino patrons who were classified as "social gamblers," "problem gamblers," and "severe problem gamblers." They were further divided into two groups on the basis of the frequency with which they visited casinos. "Regular casino patrons" were those who visited a casino once a week or more, and "nonregular casino patrons" were those who visited casinos less than once a week. One striking finding of the study was that 7 percent of regular patrons accounted for 63 percent of all visits to British casinos annually. For the *regular* patrons, the *severe problem gambling* rate was 8.1 percent compared with 1.7 percent for the *nonregular* patrons. Regular patrons also had a slightly higher rate of *problem gambling* (6.7 percent) compared with nonregular patrons (5.1 percent) (Fisher, 2000).

Both of these studies suggest that the prevalence of problem gambling is higher among the patrons of gambling venues than it is in the general population and (based on the British study) that frequent (at least weekly) gambling is associated with more severe gambling problems. Susan Fisher, the author of the British study, suggests that on any given night one in six or seven patrons of British casinos are problem gamblers and that at least half of those problem gamblers have severe gambling problems (Fisher, 2000a).

THE PREVALENCE OF PROBLEM GAMBLING
IN OTHER SOCIETIES

In addition to the prevalence studies that have been done in the United States, similar research has been done in other societies.

In *Canada*, prevalence studies have been carried out in six of the ten Provinces. All the research has been done between 1989 and 1996 and used the South Oaks Gambling Screen or modifications of it. Using the same (or very similar) scoring criteria used in studies done in the United States, the prevalence of problem gambling in Canada seems to be quite similar to that in the United States. For example, in Quebec and Saskatchewan *lifetime* prevalence rates of 3.8 and 4.0 percent, respectively, were found. In New Brunswick, Nova Scotia, Alberta, and Saskatchewan, using responses *for the past year*, problem gambling prevalence rates of 4.5, 4.7, 5.4, and 2.7 percent, respectively, were found. In the survey conducted in Ontario, it is not clear whether the time frame used was lifetime or past year. In this case, a prevalence rate of 8.6 percent was reported (Ladouceur, 1996).

Prevalence studies have also been carried out in *Australia* and *New Zealand.* In Australia, a 1991 survey of 2,744 people in four state capitals (Sydney, Melbourne, Adelaide, and Brisbane) concluded that problem gamblers constituted 1.16 percent of the population. This relatively low prevalence rate is not entirely comparable to the findings of studies done in the United States, because respondents were asked to answer the questions on the South Oaks Gambling screen using *the past six months* as their time frame(Dickerson et al., 1996).

In New Zealand, a 1991 survey of 3,933 people found a somewhat higher rate of problem gambling. Using the *past six months* timeframe, 3.3 percent of the New Zealand population can be considered problem gamblers. However, when *lifetime* problem gambling was assessed, the prevalence rate was 6.9 percent, a figure consistent with the results of research done in the United States (Abbott and Volberg, 1996).

Research on the prevalence of compulsive gambling has also been done in *Spain* in the early 1990s using the South Oaks Gambling Screen. On the basis of studies conducted in four regions of the country, the rate of problem gambling (scores of three or higher on the South Oaks Gambling Screen) seems to be about 4 percent (Becona, 1996).

Although no prevalence surveys comparable to those discussed thus far have been done in other European countries, for Germany and Holland other information exists that is suggestive of the existence of problem gambling in these countries. In the *German* state of Bavaria, for example, 30,000 people have banned *themselves* from casinos. In 1987, 3,400 people attended Gamblers Anonymous meetings throughout the country, and in 1988 4,900 people with problems related to slot machine gambling sought advice or treatment from Gamblers Anonymous (Becona, 1996),

Data of a somewhat more indirect sort from *Holland* suggest that problem gambling occurs in that society too. There are 17 alcohol and drug treatment centers located throughout Holland. The number of people seeking help at these centers for gambling-related problems rose from 10 in 1985 to 3,883 in 1991 (Becona, 1996).

In late 1997, Shaffer et al. (1997) completed a review of 120 published and unpublished prevalence studies conducted in the United States and Canada. They analyzed studies of the general population and "special populations" such as prisoners, college students, and youth. Shaffer et al. distinguish between level 1, level 2, and level 3 gamblers. Level 1 refers to people who gamble with no adverse consequences. Level 2 gamblers are people whose gambling produces a range of adverse consequences, but they do not meet the criteria for level 3. At level 3 are gamblers who meet the diagnostic criteria for pathological gambling. Shaffer et al. refer to these as "disordered gamblers". They concluded that, on the basis of *lifetime* prevalence, disordered (level 3) gamblers make up 1.60 percent of the general adult population. For level 2 gambling, the lifetime prevalence rate was 3.85 percent in the general adult population. This review also concluded that the rate of disordered (level 3) gambling has been increasing over time.

THE SOCIAL AND DEMOGRAPHIC DISTRIBUTION OF PROBLEM GAMBLING

How is problem gambling related to social and demographic factors such as age, gender, race/ethnicity, and indicators of socioeconomic status? This section addresses this question. In terms of age, problem gambling among youth and the elderly has received a good deal of attention in recent years. What we know about these two extremes of the age continuum will be dealt with first.

Gambling Among Youth

In most jurisdictions it is illegal for anyone younger than the age of 18 to gamble, and in some states the age at which people can gamble legally is 21. Yet, gambling is commonplace among young people. After reviewing 14 U.S. and six Canadian studies, Jacobs (2000) concluded that gambling by middle and high school students is both very prevalent and increasing. In the U.S. studies conducted between 1984 and 1988, 45 percent of students indicated that they had gambled for money during the past year, with a range from 20 to 86 percent (Jacobs et al., 1985, 1987; Kuley and Jacobs, 1987; Lesieur and Klein, 1984; Steinberg, 1984). Studies conducted between 1989 and 1999 reported an average past year gambling rate of 66 percent, with a range from 52 to 71 percent (Kuley and Jacobs, 1989; Shaffer et al., 1994; Volberg, 1993, 1996; Volberg and Moore, 1998; Wallish, 1993,

1995; Westphal et al., 1998; Winters et al., 1990). The Canadian studies, all conducted between 1988 and 1998, found a past year gambling rate of 66 percent (identical to the U.S. rate for the comparable time period), with a range from 60 to 91 percent (Gupta and Derevensky, 1998; Insight Canada, 1994; Ladouceur and Mireault, 1988; Omnifacts Research Limited, 1993; Rupcich et al., in press; and Wynne et al., 1996).

What kinds of gambling games do young people play? The answer is "Just about every legal and illegal game that adults play." The studies reviewed by Jacobs (2000) report that the most popular forms of gambling are *first*, cards, dice, and board games with family and friends; *second*, games of personal skill played with age peers, *third*, sports betting, mostly with peers in school but also with bookies, and *fourth*, bingo. There is one caveat to this preference order; when state or provincial lotteries were operating before the study was conducted, lottery games, especially pull-tab and scratch-off games, were the favorite form of gambling.

In the late 1980s a survey of 1,771 students at five colleges found that more than 90 percent of the males and 82 percent of the females had gambled at some time in their lives. About a third of the males and 15 percent of the females gambled at least once a week (Lesieur et al., 1991).

Research on youth gambling has found consistent gender differences in gambling behavior. Compared to girls, boys begin gambling earlier, gamble on a greater variety of games and activities, gamble more often, and spend more time and money gambling. If gambling games are arranged on a continuum ranging from skill and knowledge at one end and pure luck at the other, boys' gambling preferences cluster at the skill/knowledge end (card and board games, shooting hoops and pool, sports betting), whereas girls' preferences reflect the pure luck end (raffles, bingo, lotteries, and pull-tabs) (Jacobs, 2000).

Problem Gambling Among Youth

Numerous studies have been done of problem gambling among young people. One difficulty in studying problem gambling among youth is the fact that the standard screening instruments have been created to measure problem gambling among adults. Consequently, questions posed to young people have had to be reworded. Several youth-focused screening instruments have been developed by modifying questions in the standard (adult) versions. Research done using these instruments has found "probable pathological gambling" rate ranging between 4.7 and 8.4 percent (Derevensky and Gupta, 2000; Fisher, 2000b), and "problem gambling" rates between 0.9 and 8.7 percent (Fisher, 2000b; Poulin, 2000).

A review of the research literature by Jacobs (2000) concluded that in studies conducted between 1984 and 1988, about 10 percent of adolescents in the United States had "serious gambling-related problems." For the studies conducted between 1989 and 1999, the rate was 14 percent, suggesting an increase in serious gambling-related problems over time. In the Canadian studies reviewed by Jacobs (conducted between 1988 and 1998), the rate of serious gambling-related problems was 15 percent. Lesieur et al. (1991) reported that the level of compulsive gambling among college students was eight times higher than it was in the general adult population.

A Canadian study conducted in the late 1990s surveyed 817 Montreal high school students between the ages of 12 and 17. Using questions based on the DSM-IV specially worded to apply to adolescents, the study found that 4.7 percent were pathological gamblers and an additional 3.3 percent were problem gamblers. Eighty percent of the students had gambled during the past year, and 35 percent gambled at least once per week. Gambling was much more common than cigarette smoking, alcohol consumption, and the use of illegal drugs (Gupta and Derevensky, 1998).

Shaffer and Hall (1996) have conducted a review and synthesis of 11 studies of adolescents in five major regions of the United States and Canada. Although the studies they reviewed used different measures (DSM criteria, GA's 20 Questions, SOGS-RA) and terminology, they conclude that the rate of compulsive/pathological/problem gambling among adolescents ranges between a low of 0.9 percent (Washington state) and a high of 8.7 percent (Minnesota). On the basis of five of the studies reviewed, they concluded that there is an additional subgroup of young people who are "at risk" or have a "high risk" of developing a serious gambling problem. That group ranges in size from 9 percent to 17 percent.

The review of 120 prevalence studies discussed earlier in this chapter on adult prevalence rates also analyzed studies of prevalence rates among college students and other youth (Shaffer et al., 1997). The review concluded that the rate of level 3 "disordered" gambling was 4.67 percent among college students and 3.88 percent among youth. The prevalence rate for gambling at what the review calls "level 2" (gambling with adverse consequences but not meeting the diagnostic criteria for pathological gambling found at level 3) was 9.28 percent among college students and 9.45 percent among youth.

Some research suggests that risk-taking behavior is associated with sensation-seeking among children and adolescents. In a study of 115 third through eighth graders, Miller and Byrnes (1997) found that students who scored high on measures of thrill- and adventure-seeking were more likely to select the riskiest options in both tasks involving skill and games involving chance.This relationship held at all grade levels and was not related to gender or competitiveness. Other research suggests that gambling is part of a broader array of "deviant behaviors" that include frequent tobacco and alcohol use, physical violence, vandalism, shoplifting, and truancy (Stinchfield, 2000).

A dearth of research on gambling among college student athletes exists. One study that did investigate this found that student athletes who gambled were more likely to have attitudes supportive of risk-taking behavior in general compared with student athletes who did not gamble (Cross et al., 1998).

The 1998 NORC study provides a somewhat different picture of adolescent gambling. A survey of gambling behavior and problem gambling among 16- and 17-year-olds was conducted as part of the larger study for the National Gambling Impact Study Commission. It should be noted that this study covered a much narrower age range than most studies of problem gambling among adolescents. Using telephone interviews, 534 randomly selected 16- and 17-year-olds were surveyed. Several important findings emerged from this survey. Adolescents gamble much less frequently than adults. About a third reported that they had never gambled. Most of the gambling reported was "private gambling," especially betting on games of skill and card games. A little more than 28 percent of the 16- and 17-year-olds reported engaging in this type of gambling during the past year. Other forms of gambling reported included buying lottery tickets (13.1 percent), playing bingo (5.5 percent), betting at racetracks (2.2 percent), and gambling in casinos (1.1 percent). The survey also found that about 1.5 percent could be classified as problem or pathological gamblers, a much lower rate than was found for adults (National Opinion Research Center, 1999:61-64).

How do adolescent problem and pathological gamblers differ from their nongambling peers and their gambling peers who are not problem or pathological gamblers? A review of the adolescent gambling literature by Gupta and Derevensky (2000) reached the following conclusions and generalizations: Adolescent *pathological* gamblers are more likely than other adolescents to be risk-takers, and they have lower self-esteem compared with other adolescents. Compared with other adolescents, those who are *problem* gamblers have higher rates of depression; are more likely to experience dissociation; are more at risk of developing other addictions, score higher on excitability, extroversion, and anxiety; and score lower on conformity and self-discipline. Adolescent problem and pathological gamblers have higher rates of deviant behavior (such as delinquency and crime), disrupted family relationships, and lower academic performance.

Alcohol and drug use among youth have been the focus of a great deal of attention in recent years, including research, legislation, treatment programs, and education programs. However, comparatively little attention have been given to adolescent problem gambling. Just as getting served in a bar is exciting and gains prestige among peers, so does gambling at a casino or racetrack. In many respects, gambling has been added to alcohol and drug use in the youth culture as part of the rite of passage to adulthood (Winters and Anderson, 2000). Like getting a driver's license, getting a job, or purchasing and consuming alcohol and tobacco, gambling is an activity that symbolizes the attainment of adult status. Information about gambling's addiction potential is likely to be regarded by young people as "just another lecture" or "just say no" campaign about not doing things that adults can do. Although parents and other authority figures say you shouldn't gamble, its risky and exciting, and you can brag to your friends about having done it. Like experimentation with other exciting and risky behaviors, it should come as no surprise that gambling is an attractive and appealing activity for many young people (Winters et al., 1993). Like the adults whose behavior they may seek to emulate, young people develop similar gambling problems.

One question that has been raised by researchers studying youth gambling is whether there is a relationship between gambling (especially playing machine games) and playing video games and using the internet. The answer seems to be yes (see Griffiths and Wood, 2000 for a review of the relevant research). Video games, the internet, and gambling machines share a fundamentally similar technology, including the way the player responds to stimuli, the encouraging of total concentration, the speed of play, the aural and visual stimuli involved, the provision of incremental rewards for correct play or "wins," visual display of points or credits, and the opportunity for peer attention and approval (Griffiths and Wood, 2000). It is reasonable to conclude that gambling (especially on machine games such as slots and video poker) will become increasingly popular among young people as more and more of them become adept at using the internet and playing video games. In a sense, the internet and video games develop orientations and skills that are readily transferrable to gambling machines.

Gambling Among the Elderly

How does the gambling participation of elderly people compare with that of younger people? In 1975, people 65 and older had a *lifetime* gambling participation rate of only 35 percent compared with a rate of 67 percent of those in the 45-64 age group, 74 percent for those age 25-44, and 75 percent for those age 18-24. By 1998, the elderly had caught up to younger people. Their participation rate of 80 percent was identical to that of people age 18-24, and only 8 percentage points lower than those in the two intermediate age groups (National Opinion Research Center et al., 1999). This is a striking, dramatic indicator of increased participation in gambling by the elderly.

Past-year gambling participation by the elderly has also undergone a significant change, albeit less dramatic than for lifetime participation. In 1975, 23 percent of those 65 years of age and over had gambled during the past year compared with 60 percent of those age 45-64, 69 percent of those age 25-44, and 73 percent of those age 18-24. By 1998, the elderly had closed the gap considerably. Fifty percent of the elderly had gambled during the past year compared with the younger age groups, which ranged from 64 to 67 percent (National Opinion Research Center, et.al. 1999).

Problem Gambling Among the Elderly

The most recent national data on the relationship between age and the prevalence of problem gambling come from the survey done in

1998 by NORC for the NGISC. These data are presented in Table 4.2. A special screening instrument (the NODS) developed specifically for this survey was designed to capture the DSM-IV criteria for pathological gambling. In Table 4.2, "at-risk" gamblers are people who met one or two of the DSM criteria; "problem" gamblers are those who met three or four criteria; and "pathological" gamblers are those who met five or more criteria.

TABLE 4.2
LIFETIME AND PAST-YEAR PREVALENCE OF GAMBLING PROBLEMS, BY AGE, IN PERCENT

Age	At Risk (N = 267) Life/Year		Problem (N = 56) Life/Year		Pathological (N = 67) Life/Year	
18-29	10.1	3.9	2.1	1.0	1.3	0.3
30-39	6.9	2.1	1.5	0.8	1.0	0.6
40-49	8.9	3.3	1.9	0.7	1.4	0.8
50-64	6.1	3.6	1.2	0.3	2.2	0.9
65+	6.1	1.7	0.7	0.6	0.4	0.2

Source: National Opinion Research Center, Gemini Research, The Lewin Group and Christiansen/Cummings Associates: *Gambling Impact and Behavior Study: Report to the National Gambling Impact Study Commission*, www.norc.uchicago.edu, downloaded April 1, 1999, Table 7, pp. 26 and 27.

As one would expect, lifetime rates for all levels of gambling problems and all age groups are higher than past year rates. Although the relationship is not a perfect one, it is generally the case that prevalence rates decrease as age increases. This is consistent with the results of earlier research done in particular states. Several things stand out regarding people older than 65. The proportion of at risk gamblers (lifetime rate) among those older than 65 is the same as for those age 50-64. The proportion of problem gamblers (past year rate) is higher among those older than 65 than for those age 50-64. Among those with the most serious gambling problems (i.e., pathological) based on past year behavior, those older than 65 more closely resemble the 18-29 age group than the intermediate age groups.

Although data on prevalence rates for the elderly are not available for men and women separately, other data in the NORC survey are suggestive of the dynamics of the development of gambling problems.

Prevalence rates for men are consistently higher than those for women (see pages 82 and 83). This is in all likelihood because, compared with men, women are relative newcomers to commercial, legal gambling. An interesting relationship also exists between marital status and some prevalence rates. Widowed people have a higher past year at-risk rate than married or cohabiting people, but a lower rate than divorced, separated, or never married people (see later). Although widowed people are found in all age groups, they are more likely to be found among those older than 65, suggesting that widowhood may play a role in the development of at least some gambling problems among the elderly.

Triggers and At-Risk Factors Among the Elderly

There is no reason to believe that the gambling careers of elderly people who develop gambling problems differ dramatically from the description presented earlier. However, several distinctive features of the lives of older people make the development of gambling problems somewhat different from the way these problems develop among younger people. It is useful to think of these as "triggers" or special predisposing factors.

One important factor is *opportunity*. Regardless of where they live, legal gambling is more readily available to elderly people that it has been in the recent past. For example, in 1976 only 13 states had lotteries, two (Nevada and New York) had off-track wagering, and Nevada was the only state with casinos. By 1999, every state except Utah, Hawaii, and Tennessee had legal gambling.Thirty-seven states had lotteries, 21 had casinos, and 39 had off-track wagering. Of course, gambling has become more available to everyone, not just the elderly. During 1998, at least one person from 29 percent of all U.S. households visited a casino, producing a total of 161 million casino visits (American Gaming Association, 1999). In 1998, $677.4 billion was legally wagered, and the gambling industry had gross revenues of $54.4 billion. Between 1982 and 1998, the amount of money wagered grew by an average annual rate of 11 percent (Christiansen, 1999).

The "sunbelt" states to which elderly people have retired have developed gambling venues that also have increased the opportunity for older people to gamble. Arizona and California both have Native

American reservation casinos, and their proximity to Nevada makes for easy access to the world's premier gambling destination, Las Vegas. In Florida, elderly retirees have horse and dog racing, Jai Alai, Native American Reservation casinos, and a concentration of "cruises to nowhere." Nationally, nearly $3.9 billion was wagered in 1998 on these floating casinos that provide gambling once they are in international waters (Christiansen, 1999).

Boredom is also a trigger that leads many older people to gamble. Gambling is a way of filling the abundant leisure time that many older people find themselves with after retirement. Getting away from boring activities, relaxation, passing time, and just getting away for the day are important motivations for gambling among older people (McNeilly and Burke, 2000). Elderly people with physical limitations may be limited in the kinds of activities in which they can engage. Gambling is a relatively passive leisure activity. It has become commonplace in recent years for casinos to provide "handicapped only" blackjack tables that accommodate wheelchairs.

For older people experiencing *loneliness* or *isolation* as a result of the loss of a spouse or close friends, gambling is a way of being around and interacting with other people. Gambling venues, especially casinos, are exciting, fun places. Getting out and being around other people can be a powerful motivation to engage in gambling. Gambling may give people the feeling of being part of something rather than focusing on their isolation. To the extent that it provides a diversion from routines, gambling can be very appealing to older people.

Gambling is a marvelous *escape*. It is a fantasy world in which one can leave behind whatever problems one may want to forget about—poor health, loss of a spouse, etc. Casinos in particular facilitate the creation of a fantasy world. It is no accident that clocks and windows are hard to find in them. Initially at least, gambling for many people may be an effective solution to whatever problems they are trying to escape from.

Another reason why gambling has become popular among the elderly is the *gambling industry's marketing practices*. There is no doubt that older people are a "target market." Free admission to race tracks and free or very low-cost transportation to casinos are among the many promotions used by casinos to attract older customers. The use of "comps" (complimentary meals, lodging, gifts, etc.) is widespread. Casino operators have also developed hospitality programs that emphasize making older people feel welcome and catering to their interests and needs.

To illustrate the development of problem gambling among older people, two case studies are presented. Their experiences are fairly typical. Both are based on people that the author has dealt with. In the interest of maintaining privacy, they have been given fictitious names, and some of the details of their lives have been altered.

CASE STUDY ONE

Hooked on Bingo

In her early 60s when her husband Phil retired, Lena was looking forward to "doing things." But Phil, whom she described as a "couch potato," had other ideas. Watching TV and napping was his idea of the good life.

When some friends suggested she go with them to play bingo at a local church, she jumped at the chance to get out. Bingo was fun and an escape from boredom. At first she won a little money, but before long she was losing more than winning. The weekly game turned into a biweekly game, and soon she was going to every game she could find, often to several a day.

Lena and Phil had limited financial resources, and soon money to gamble with became a problem. Although credit card solicitations are viewed by most people as a nuisance, Lena welcomed them. In addition to maxing out the credit line on about a dozen cards, she got a home equity loan on the home. Oblivious to what she was doing, Phil would "sign anything I put in front of him."

She reached a point where she had about $100,000 in credit card and home equity loan payments due and no way to pay them. Lena had a part-time job as an accountant at a construction company. She "borrowed" (i.e., embezzled) $75,000, was caught, and arrested.She pleaded guilty and was looking at about 10 years in jail.

Her lawyer got her into Gamblers Anonymous hoping to convince the court that she recognized the seriousness of her addiction and was doing something about it. It worked. She got a suspended sentence with 10 years probation. A plan for repaying the construction company was worked out.

When I met Lena, she had been "clean" for a little over three years. She was getting individual counseling and regularly attending GA meetings. She also spends a good deal of time talking to older people about the addiction potential of gambling. (*Source*: From the author's files.)

CASE STUDY TWO

No Easy Solution

Bill had been a gambler and salesman all his life. His gambling involved betting on horse races and sporting events, with an occasional trip to a casino. His gambling usually involved small amounts of money well within his budget. That changed when his wife died at the age of 64.

Bill, 67, found himself alone, depressed, and looking at an unknown future. Still working in sales, he was "on the road" a good deal, working with minimal supervision. Continuing to make bets through his bookie, he also spent an increasing amount of time at racetracks and casinos throughout the upper Midwest as he traveled on his job. Gambling was a great escape for him, and before long the job was secondary to gambling.

Within a year, Bill had gone through about $150,000, his total life savings. At one point he owed his bookie about $20,000. Bill learned about GA after calling an "800 Helpline" number posted at a riverboat casino in Illinois. He began attending meetings, got into group counseling with a certified gambling counselor, and had been in recovery about 3 years when I met him.

Over the next five years, Bill tried gambling in a "controlled" way. It didn't work. He dropped out of GA and the counseling group and began spending more and more time at casinos. During these five years, he was in and out of GA at least three times. The last I heard (about two years ago) he was back gambling. He knows he has a problem, but he just can't deal with it. Whether he will ever fully deal with his addiction is uncertain. (*Source*: From the author's files.)

PROBLEM GAMBLING AND OTHER DEMOGRAPHIC VARIABLES

Gender

Until quite recently, men have been much more involved in gambling than have women. The expansion of legal gambling since the 1970s has changed that considerably. The two national surveys discussed earlier (conducted in 1975 and 1989) provide evidence that the gambling gender gap is closing. In 1975, 61 percent of women indicated that they had gambled at some time in their lives compared with 75 percent of men. By 1998, the figure was up to 83 percent for women compared with 88 percent for men. A similar pattern exists for *past-year* gambling. Between 1975 and 1998, the percentage of past-year female gamblers rose from 55 to 60 percent, whereas the rate for men decreased very slightly, from 68 to 67 percent.

The 1998 NORC survey found a strong relationship between gender and problem gambling. The proportion of men and women who are pathological, problem, and at-risk gamblers based on *lifetime* measures is presented in Table 4.3. For all three levels of gambling problems, men have a higher rate than women. Men are twice as likely as women to be pathological or problem gamblers.

Race/Ethnicity

Compared with Caucasians, African-Americans are more likely to be pathological, problem, and at risk gamblers (see Table 4.3). They have the highest rate of pathological gambling, about three times that of Caucasians. Although Hispanics have the lowest rate of pathological and problem gambling, they have the largest proportion of at-risk gamblers. Ironically, African-Americans and Hispanics tend to be underrepresented at Gamblers Anonymous meetings.

TABLE 4.3
LIFETIME PREVALENCE OF GAMBLING PROBLEMS, BY GENDER,
RACE/ETHNICITY, EDUCATION,   INCOME, AND MARITAL STATUS, IN PERCENT

	At Risk (N=267)	Problem (N=56)	Pathological (N=67)
Gender			
Men	9.6	2.0	1.7
Women	6.0	1.1	0.8
Race/ethnicity			
Caucasian	6.8	1.4	1.0
Black	9.2	2.7	3.2
Hispanic	12.7	0.9	0.5
Other	8.8	1.2	0.9
Education			
Less than HS	10.0	1.7	2.1
HS graduate	8.0	2.2	1.9
Some college	7.9	1.5	1.1
College grad	6.4	0.8	0.5

Income

Less than $24,000	7.3	1.6	1.7
$24,000-49,999	6.9	1.8	1.4
$50,000-99,999	8.0	1.3	0.9
$100,000+	13.4	1.4	0.7

Marital status

Married	5.9	1.0	1.0
Divorced/separated	9.9	1.7	3.0
Never married	11.4	2.6	1.2
Cohabiting	6.8	1.2	0.8
Widowed	7.3	0.5	0.0

Source: National Opinion Research Center, Gemini Research, The Lewin Group and Christiansen/ Cummings Associates: *Gambling Impact and Behavior Study: Report to the National Gambling Impact Study Commission*, www.norc.uchicago.edu, downloaded April 1, 1999, Table 7, pp. 26 and 27.

Education

The amount of formal education that people have is inversely related to the likelihood that they are pathological or at risk gamblers (see Table 4.3). In both cases, as education increases, the proportion of pathological and at-risk gambling decreases. However, this pattern does not hold for problem gambling, in which the highest rate occurs among high school graduates.

Income

The data in Table 4.3 on the relationship between income and gambling problems are somewhat surprising. Because education and income are strongly correlated, we would expect to see rates of pathological, problem, and at-risk gambling related to income in the same way they are related to education. This turns out to not be the case. Pathological gambling does decrease as income increases, but the relationship is not consistent for problem gambling. The proportion of people classified as at-risk gamblers is higher among those with annual incomes more than $50,000 compared with those with incomes less than $50,000 and is actually the highest among those with incomes of $100,000 and over.

Marital Status

The highest rate of pathological gambling occurs among divorced and separated people. However, those who have never been married have the highest rate of problem and at-risk gambling (see Table 4.3). The proportion of married people with any degree of gambling problem is lower than it is for divorced/separated, never married, or cohabiting people. Widowed people have the lowest rate of pathological and problem gambling, but they are a little more likely than married people to be at-risk gamblers.

PREVALENCE AND PROXIMITY TO LEGAL GAMBLING

In the 1998 NORC survey, data were collected on two items that bear on the issue of what effect proximity to gambling facilities has on the development of gambling problems. Respondents were asked if they lived in a state with or without a lottery, and they were asked to estimate the distance between their place of residence and the nearest casino.

Those living in states without a lottery actually had a slightly higher rate of pathological gambling compared with those in states with a lottery (1.5 percent compared with 1.2 percent). In the case of problem gambling, the rates were virtually the same (1.4 percent for those living in states without a lottery and 1.5 percent among those in states with a lottery). However, at-risk gambling was substantially higher among people living in states with a lottery 8.3 percent) compared with those in states without a lottery (4.6 percent) (National Opinion Research Center et al., 1999).

This finding regarding at-risk gambling needs to be interpreted cautiously. The higher level of at-risk gambling in states with a lottery does not mean that there is a causal link between the two. We do not know whether the at-risk gamblers were lottery players and, if they were, how much lottery play may have contributed to their gambling problem. Undoubtedly, some at-risk gamblers live in states with lotteries and may play the lottery minimally (or not at all), and their gambling problem is related to other forms of gambling (e.g., racing, bingo, casino games, legal or illegal sports betting).

The distance from peoples' residence and the nearest casino shows a modest relationship to the prevalence of some gambling problems. Those living within 50 miles of a casino are more likely to be pathological gamblers than those living 51 to 250 miles from a casino (2.1 compared with 0.9 percent). However, those living more than 250 miles from a casino have a rate of pathological gambling of 1.3 percent. The rate of problem gambling is 2.3 percent for those living within 50 miles of a casino, higher than the 1.2 percent found among those living 51 to 250 and more than 250 miles from a casino. The highest rate of at-risk gambling occurs among those living 51 to 250 miles from a casino (8.5 percent). The rate of at risk gambling is lower among those living within 50 miles of a casino (7.4 percent), and lowest for those who live more than 250 miles from a casino (5.5 percent) (National Opinion Research Center et al., 1999).

Like the findings on prevalence and the presence of a lottery in one's state of residence, these findings on proximity to a casino need to be interpreted carefully. They do not establish a causal connection between prevalence and how close people live to a casino. We do not know that the pathological and problem gamblers who lived closest to a casino actually gambled at those nearby casinos. Similarly, we do not know whether casino gamblers played casino games exclusively or how much casino gambling may have contributed to their gambling problems (if at all) compared with other forms of gambling.

SELF-CONCEPTION: A CAVEAT

One final item from the 1998 NORC survey deserves a brief mention. About 1 percent of the respondents to the survey identified themselves as "professional gamblers." It is by no means clear what that self-description means. These are in all likelihood not people whose main occupation is that of gambler. It may mean that they gamble a lot, generally win, or know (or think they know) how to play different gambling games well. At any rate, it is interesting that a strikingly high 19.8 percent of these self-defined "professional gamblers" scored as pathological gamblers on the NODS. Only 2 percent were problem gamblers, but a comparatively high 19.2 percent were at-risk gamblers (National Opinion Research Center et al., 1999).

PREVALENCE OF PROBLEM GAMBLING COMPARED TO OTHER DISORDERS

How does problem gambling compare to other disorders such as alcohol and other drug dependence? Using the estimates for pathological and problem gambling from the 1998 NORC survey, the prevalence of alcohol and other drug problems appears to be considerably lower. For comparison purposes, these prevalence rates are presented in Table 4.4.

TABLE 4.4
PREVALENCE OF PROBLEM GAMBLING AND OTHER DISORDERS, IN PERCENT

	Past year	*Lifetime*
Problem and pathological gambling	1.3	2.7
Alcohol dependence	7.2	14.1
Other drug dependence	2.8	7.5

Sources: National Opinion Research Center, Gemini Research, The Lewin Group and Christiansen/ Cummings Associates, *Gambling Impact and Behavior Study: Report to the National Gambling Impact Study Commission*, www.norc.uchicago.edu, downloaded April 1, 1999, Table 6, p. 25 and Korn, David A., and Shaffer, Howard J.: Gambling and the health of the public: Adopting a public health perspective. *Journal of Gambling Studies, 15*:289-365, 1999.

Clearly, alcohol dependence is much more prevalent than problem and pathological gambling for both past year and lifetime rates. In terms of past-year prevalence, dependence on drugs other than alcohol is only slightly more prevalent than problem and pathological gambling. However, the lifetime problem and pathological gambling prevalence rate is considerably lower than the lifetime rate for drugs other than alcohol.

SUMMARY

Both national and state studies are available for estimating the prevalence of problem gambling. The most comprehensive and recent national research estimates that 1.2 percent of the adult population are "pathological" gamblers, 1.5 percent are "problem" gamblers, and 7.7 percent are "at-risk" gamblers with the potential of becoming problem or pathological gamblers.

A number of demographic variables are related to the prevalence of problem gambling. Men are more likely than women to be problem gamblers. Pathological, problem, and at-risk gambling occurs at a higher rate among African-Americans than among Caucasians. Hispanics have the lowest rate of pathological and problem gambling but the highest rate of at-risk gambling.

Education and income are not consistently related to the prevalence of gambling problems. However, it is clear that the prevalence of gambling problems is lower for married and widowed people than for those who are divorced or never married.

Gambling among adolescents is widespread. Research on the rate of problem gambling among youth is mixed, with some findings indicating that it is higher than for adults and other research reporting that it is comparable to adults. Older adults (especially those over age 65) gamble much more frequently today than they did in the mid-1970s when legal gambling was less available. However, their rate of problem gambling seems to be comparable to that of the overall adult population.

A final factor related to the prevalence of problem gambling is proximity to gambling venues. In general, the closer people live to casinos, the higher the rate of problem gambling.

REFERENCES

Abbott, Max W., and Volberg, Rachel A.: The New Zealand national survey of problem and pathological gambling. Journal od Gambling Studies, 12: 143-160, 1996.

Becona, Elisardo: Prevalence surveys of problem and pathological gambling in Europe: The cases of Germany, Holland, and Spain. *Journal of Gambling Studies, 12*:179-192, 1996.

Cross, Michael E., Basten, Jay, Hendrick, Erin Marie, Kristofic, Brian, and Schaffer, Evan J.: Student-athletes and gambling: An analysis of attitudes towards risk-taking. *Journal of Gambling Studies, 14*:431-439, 1998.

Derevensky, Jeffrey L., and Gupta, Rina: Prevalence estimates of adolescent gambling: A comparison of the SOGS-RA, DSM-IV-J, and the GA 20 questions. *Journal of Gambling Studies, 16*:227-251, 2000.

Dickerson, Mark G., Baron, Ellen, Hong, Sung-Mook, and Cottrell, David: Estimating the extent and degree of gambling related problems in the Australian population: A national survey. *Journal of Gambling Studies, 12*:161-178, 1996.

Fisher, Susan: Measuring the prevalence of sector-specific problem gambling: A study of casino patrons. *Journal of Gambling Studies,* 25-51, 2000a.

Fisher, Sue: Developing the DSM-IV-DSM-IV criteria to identify adolescent problem gambling in non-clinical populations. *Journal of Gambling Studies, 16*:253-273, 2000b.

Griffiths, Mark, and Wood, Richard T. A.: Risk factors in adolescence: The case of gambling, videogame playing, and the internet. *Journal of Gambling Studies, 16*: 199-225, 2000.

Gupta, Rina, and Derevensky, Jeffrey L.: Adolescent gambling behavior: A prevalence study and examination of the correlates associated with problem gambling. *Journal of Gambling Studies, 14*:319-345, 1998.

Gupta, Rina, and Derevensky, Jeffrey L.: Adolescents with gambling problems: From research to treatment. *Journal of Gambling Studies. 16*:315-342, 2000.

Insight Research Limited: *An Exploration of the Prevalence of Pathological Gambling Behavior Among Adolescents in Ontario.* Report Prepared for the Canadian Foundation on Compulsive Gambling, Toronto: Insight Research Limited, 1994.

Jacobs, Durand F.: Juvenile gambling in North America: An analysis of long term trends and future prospects. *Journal of Gambling Studies, 16*:119-152, 2000.

Jacobs, Durand F., Marston, A.R., and Singer, R.D.: Study of gambling and other health-threatening behaviors among high school students. Unpublished manuscript, Loma Linda, CA: Jerry L. Pettis Memorial Veterans Hospital, 1985.

Jacobs, Durand F., Marston, A.R., and Singer, R.D.: A post-lottery study of gambling behaviors among high school students. Unpublished manuscript, Loma Linda, CA: Jerry L. Pettis Memorial Veterans Hospital, 1987.

Kallick, M., et. al.: *A Survey of American Gambling Attitudes and Behavior.* Research Report Series, Survey Research Center, Institute for Social Research, Ann Arbor: University of Michigan Press, 1979.

Kuley, N., and Jacobs, Durand F.: A pre-lottery benchmark study of teenage gambling in Virginia. Unpublished manuscript, Loma Linda, CA: Loma Linda University Department of Psychiatry, 1987.

Kuley, N., and Jacobs, Durand F.: A post-lottery impact study of effects on teenage gambling behaviors. Unpublished manuscript, Loma Linda, CA: Loma Linda University Department of Psychiatry, 1989.

Ladouceur, Robert: The prevalence of pathological gambling in Canada. *Journal of Gambling Studies, 12*:129-142, 1996.

Ladouceur, Robert, and Mireault, Chantal: Gambling behaviors among high school students in the Quebec area. *Journal of Gambling Behavior, 4*:3-12, 1988.

Lesieur, Henry R., Cross, J., Frank, M., Welch, M., and Mark, M.: Gambling and pathological gambling among university students. *Addictive Behaviors, 16*:517-527, 1991.

Lesieur, Henry R., and Klein, Robert: Gambling among high school students in New Jersey. Unpublished manuscript, New York: John Jay College, 1984.

McNeilly, Dennis P. and Burke, William J.: Late life gambling: The attitudes and behaviors of older adults. *Journal of Gambling Studies, 16*:393-415, 2000.

Miller, D.C., and Byrnes, J.P.: The role of contextual and personal factors in children's risk taking. *Developmental Psychology, 33*:814-823, 1997.

National Opinion Research Center, Gemini Research, The Lewin Group, and Christiansen/ Cummings Associates: *Gambling Impact and Behavior Study: Report to the National Gambling Impact Study Commission,* www. norc.uchicago.edu, downloaded April 1, 1999.

Omnifacts Research Limited: *An Examination of the Prevalence of Gambling in Nova Scotia.* Research Report Number 93090 for the Nova Scotia Department of Health, Drug Dependency Services, Halifax: Omnifacts Research Limited, 1993.

Poulin, Christiane: Problem gambling among adolescent students in the atlantic provinces of Canada. *Journal of Gambling Studies, 16*:53-78, 2000.

Rupich, N., Govoni, R., and Frisch, G.: Gambling behavior of adolescent gamblers. *Journal of Gambling Studies,* (in press).

Shaffer, Howard J., and Hall, Matthew N.: Estimating the prevalence of adolescent gambling disorders: A quantitative synthesis and guide toward standard gambling nomenclature. *Journal of Gambling Studies, 12*:193-214. 1996.

Shaffer, Howard J., Hall, Matthew N., and Vander Bilt, Joni: *Estimating the Prevalence of Disordered Gambling Behavior in the United States and Canada: A Meta-Analysis,* Cambridge: MA: Harvard Medical School, 1997.

Shaffer, Howard J., LaBrie, Richard, Scanlan, Kathleen M., and Cummings, Thomas N.: Pathological gambling among adolescents: Massachusetts gambling screen (MAGS). *Journal of Gambling Studies, 10*:339-362, 1994.

Steinberg, Marvin: Gambling behavior among high school students in Connecticut. Paper presented at the Third National Conference on Gambling Behavior, New London, 1988.

Stinchfield, Randy: Gambling and correlates of gambling among Minnesota Public School Students. *Journal of Gambling Studies, 16*:153-173, 2000.

U.S. Bureau of the Census: *Statistical Abstract of the United States: 1996,* 116th Ed.). Washington, DC: Government Printing Office, 1966.

Volberg, Rachel A.: *Gambling and Problem Gambling in Washington State.* Report to the Washington State Lottery, Albany, NY: Gemini Research, 1993.

Volberg, Rachel A. and Moore, W.L.: *Gambling and Problem Gambling Among Adolescents in Washington State: A Replication Study, 1993-1999.* A Report to the Washington State Lottery, Northampton, MA: Gemini Research, 1999.

Volberg, Rachel A. and Abbott, Max W.: *Gambling and Problem Gambling Among Adolescents in Washington State: A Replication Study, 1993-1999.* A Report to the Washington State Lottery, Northampton, MA: Gemini Research, 1999.

Wallisch, Lynn S.: *Gambling in Texas: The 1992 Texas survey of adolescent gambling behavior.* Austin, TX: Texas Commission on Alcohol and Drug Abuse, 1993.

Wallisch, Lynn S.: *Gambling in Texas: The 1995 Texas survey of adolescent gambling behavior.* Austin, TX: Texas Commission on Alcohol and Drug Abuse, 1995.

Westphal, J.R., Rush, J.A., Stevens, L., and Johnson, L.J.: Pathological gambling among Louisiana students: Grades six through twelve. Paper presented at the American Psychiatric Association Annual Meeting, Toronto, 1998.

Winters, Ken C., and Anderson, Nikki: Gambling involvement and drug use among adolescents. *Journal of Gambling Studies, 16*:175-198, 2000.

Winters, Ken C., Stinchfield, Randy D., and Fulkerson, Jayne: *Adolescent Survey of Gambling Behavior in Minnesota: A Benchmark.* Report to the Department of Human Services Mental Health Division, Duluth, MN: Center for Addiction Studies, University of Minnesota, 1990.

Winters, Ken C., Stinchfield, Randy D., and Fulkerson, Jayne: Patterns and characteristics of adolescent gambling. *Journal of Gambling Studies, 9*:371-386, 1993.

Wynne, H.J., Smith, G.J., and Jacobs, Durand F.: *Adolescent Gambling and Problem Gambling in Alberta, Alberta*: Alberta Alcohol and Drug Abuse Commission, 1996.

Chapter 5

THE SOCIAL COSTS OF
PROBLEM GAMBLING

Identifying the social costs of problem gambling is a difficult task for several reasons. One very important reason is that there is a dearth of reliable data and solid research on the subject. In addition, it is difficult to measure many of the variables that fall under the broad heading of "social costs." It is even more difficult to establish a causal connection between gambling behavior and many social costs.

THE CONCEPT OF SOCIAL COST

"Social cost" is an economic concept that has been borrowed and used by people attempting to identify the costs associated with problem gambling. In strictly economic terms, "the social cost of an action is the amount by which that action reduces aggregate societal real wealth" (Walker and Barnett, 1999). As we will see, many of the consequences of problem gambling produce results (costs) to which a monetary value cannot easily be attached, if at all. How does one place a dollar value on the anguish associated with divorce, desertion, or neglect? How does one quantify and assign a dollar figure to the cost of depression that makes it difficult for a person to function on the job or meet family obligations? Many of the consequences of problem gambling might better be regarded as producing "psychic costs" rather than social costs.

Nevertheless, a variety of social costs are associated with problem gambling and are relatively easy to identify despite the difficulty of measuring them. Some of the costs that have been identified as a consequence of problem gambling include income lost from missed work; decreased productivity on the job; depression and stress-related illnesses; thinking about, attempting, and successfully committing suicide; unrecovered loans (by friends, family members, and lending institutions); unpaid debts (e.g., credit card debt); foreclosed mortgages; bankruptcies; higher insurance premiums resulting from fraudulent claims; and divorces caused by problem gambling.

For convenience, the costs associated with problem gambling will be reviewed and summarized under four broad categories: costs to individuals and their families and friends; costs to financial institutions; costs to the human service and criminal justice systems of the society; and costs to the employers of problem gamblers.

COSTS TO FAMILIES: STRESS AND CONFLICT IN THE FAMILIES OF PROBLEM GAMBLERS

The psychological costs of problem gambling to the families of problem gamblers are enormous. By the time they get to the point of seeking help for their gambling problem, problem gamblers are heavily in debt, may have lost their jobs, are likely to be experiencing depression, and have seriously considered (and possibly attempted) suicide. Depression and anxiety are commonplace reactions to gambling-related problems. They are also likely to have withdrawn from social contact with others and feel both guilty and helpless as they confront their gambling-related problems.

Several studies have found that between 21 and 36 percent of Gamblers Anonymous members have lost their jobs (Ladouceur et al., 1994; Lesieur and Anderson, 1995; Meyer et al., 1995; Thompson et al., 1996). The financial costs incurred by problem gamblers are comparably devastating. Heavily mortgaged homes and businesses; bankruptcy, money owed to friends, banks, loan companies, credit card companies, the Internal Revenue Service, loan sharks, bookies, and casinos all represent indebtedness from which there is no easy way out. Studies of members of Gamblers Anonymous indicate that from 18 to 28 percent of men and 8 percent of women have declared bankruptcy (Lesieur, 1997). Recent studies of Gamblers Anonymous members in Wisconsin and Illinois found that at the time of entering

Gamblers Anonymous they had gambling-related debts averaging $38,664 in Wisconsin and $113,640 in Illinois (Lesieur and Anderson, 1995; Thompson et al., 1996).

Having spent years (even decades) lying to family members about their gambling and financial problems, to say that problem gamblers have strained relationships with spouses, children, and other relatives is an understatement. In those marriages that do not experience divorce, spouses and children are likely to experience resentment and confusion about the material deprivations that the family may have undergone as a result of the compulsive gambler's expenditures. With compulsive gamblers' lives revolving around gambling and getting money with which to gamble, immediate family members are likely to feel ignored and rejected. They are likely to have had little to do with their spouse and children. The ex-spouse of a problem gambler described her husband (who bet mainly on college and professional football games) as "disappearing" in August as he began handicapping games for the beginning of the season and "reappearing" in February after the Pro Bowl game. Of course, he didn't really disappear, but handicapping, betting, and following the results of games was such an all-consuming activity that, for all practical purposes, he simply was not a participating member of the family.

Often as a result of financial problems and emotional absence and neglect, problem gambler's marriages experience separation or end in divorce at a very high rate. Both the emotional and financial costs of separation and divorce need to be acknowledged. Gamblers Anonymous members in Wisconsin and Illinois report that between 26 and 30 percent have experienced gambling-related divorces or separations (Lesieur and Anderson, 1995; Thompson et al., 1996). The families of compulsive gamblers are similar to those of alcoholics and other drug addicts. Problem gamblers' families are actually less cohesive and less independent than those of alcohol and other drug addicts. They function more poorly than families in the general population in terms of such things as problem solving, communication, and taking on responsibilities (Ahrons, 1989; Ciarrocchi and Hohnmann, 1989; and Epstein, 1992).

In Chapter 2, it was pointed out that problem gamblers are more likely than the general population to attempt suicide. A national study of actual suicides provides additional evidence of a link between gambling and suicide. With data from the U.S. National Center for Health

Statistics for the period 1969-91, Phillips et al. (1997) compared the Las Vegas, Reno, and Atlantic City Standard Metropolitan Statistical Areas (SMSA) with the rest of the country. They examined suicides among both visitors and residents. Nationally, the average rate of visitor suicides as a percent of all visitor deaths was 0.97 percent. For Las Vegas, the rate was 4.28 percent, the highest in the country. Reno's and Atlantic City's rates (2.31 and 1.87 percent respectively) were also well above the national average. In the case of Atlantic City, visitor suicide rates were not higher than similar communities before the opening of casinos in 1978. However, after casinos opened, visitor suicide rates became unusually high. Among *residents* during the three-year period 1989-1991, Las Vegas and Reno had the highest suicide rates in the country, and the rate for Atlantic City was significantly above the national average. This study also found no support for the interpretation that gambling settings "attract" suicidal people, either as visitors or as residents. Phillips et al. conclude that the risks of suicide are elevated for gamblers and the spouses and children of gamblers visiting gambling communities and for gamblers and their spouses and children who reside in such communities. They also cautiously point out that the increased expansion and availability of legalized gambling may be accompanied by an increase in suicides.

The wives of problem gamblers have an attempted suicide rate about three times higher than that of married women in the general population (Lorenz and Shuttlesworth, 1983). Possibly as a reaction to the frustrations of dealing with a problem gambler, about 37 percent of their spouses have physically abused their children (Lorenz, 1981).

Not a great deal is known about the children of problem gamblers. However, some research suggests that, compared with their peers, they have lower academic performance in school, are more likely to have drug, gambling, and eating disorders; and are more likely to be depressed (Jacobs, 1989; Jacobs et al., 1989b). Other research has found inconsistent support for this conclusion (Lesieur and Rothschild, 1989). Children from "multiproblem" families (including problem gambling) seem to exhibit more of these problems than those from families with only a compulsive gambling parent. Children of problem gamblers who have participated in treatment programs also are less likely to exhibit these problems than those who have not been involved in treatment and recovery programs.

COSTS TO FINANCIAL INSTITUTIONS

Banks, loan companies, credit unions, credit card issuers, and insurance companies all incur costs generated by problem gamblers. As banks and loan companies pursue unpaid loans and mortgages, financial costs are incurred. Efforts to collect payments and garnish wages, as well as foreclosure proceedings, all represent costs to those institutions. Insurance companies also incur expenses as they deal with fraudulent claims from compulsive gamblers and unpaid premiums.

COSTS TO THE HUMAN SERVICE SYSTEM: CRISES, DEPENDENCE, AND COUNSELING

When they become desperate, problem gamblers and their families may turn to human service agencies for food stamps and financial assistance through general welfare programs or programs such as Aid to Families with Dependent Children (AFDC). Unemployment and disability benefits may also be used for gambling or to pay gambling debts.

A good deal of attention has been given in recent years to "deadbeat parents" who fail to make payments for the support of their dependent children after divorce. Although information is not available on the extent to which this problem is exacerbated by problem gamblers, it seems reasonable that some of it can be attributed to them. Pursuing deadbeat parents is a cost for human service agencies in the form of the time and effort of employees spent trying to obtain payments.

COSTS TO THE CRIMINAL JUSTICE SYSTEM: CRIMINALITY AMONG PROBLEM GAMBLERS

The criminal justice system also incurs costs related to problem gambling. Problem gamblers commit crimes to get money with which to gamble and pay their debts. As already noted, a variety of "white collar" crimes are likely to be committed by them. When apprehended, the cost of trials and incarceration for those crimes is borne by the criminal justice system. Lesieur and Anderson report that in their study of 184 Gamblers Anonymous members in Illinois, 56 (30%) admitted stealing. Whereas one member admitted stealing $7,500,000, the average amount stolen was $60,700 (Lesieur and Anderson, 1995). In a Wisconsin survey of Gamblers Anonymous members, 46 percent admitted stealing, including one person who stole $8,000,000. The average amount stolen was $5,738 (Thompson et al., 1996).

COSTS TO EMPLOYERS: PROBLEM GAMBLERS AND EMPLOYEE ASSISTANCE PROGRAMS

As employees, problem gamblers create costs for their employers as a result of tardiness, absenteeism, and theft. They seek advances on their pay and may spend time trying to borrow money from coworkers. They may gamble at work and spend time on the phone with a bookie or arranging loans and trying to put off creditors. They also are likely to take extended lunch hours and breaks, especially if they work with minimal supervision. Above all, they are distracted and not likely to be conscientious, productive employees. Concentrating on their gambling and related money concerns is their first priority, not their work. Problem gamblers are also likely to contribute more than other employees to the cost of employer-sponsored health insurance premiums because of the stress-related illnesses they experience because of their gambling.

Several studies have found that between 69 and 76 percent of problem gamblers indicate that they have missed time from work (absence, tardiness) because of their gambling (Ladouceur et al., 1994; Lesieur and Anderson, 1995; Meyer et al., 1995).

FINDINGS FROM THE 1998 NORC SURVEY

The 1998 NORC survey, discussed in earlier chapters, is a major source of information about social costs. In addition to answering questions about their gambling behavior and answering questions on the NODS, the people interviewed also were asked about behaviors and experiences that bear directly on the issue of social costs.

In Table 5.1, pathological and problem gamblers are compared with low risk gamblers on several variables representing personal and social costs. An example of how to read this Table is "compared with low-risk gamblers, pathological gamblers are 2.62 times more likely to have lost a job or to have been fired during the past year."

TABLE 5.1
ODDS RATIOS OF PATHOLOGICAL AND PROBLEM GAMBLERS COMPARED
WITH LOW-RISK GAMBLERS FOR SELECTED SOCIAL COSTS

Cost variable	Level of gambling problem	
	Pathological	*Problem*
Lost a job/fired past year	2.62	2.07
Unemployment benefits, past 12 mo.	2.81	2.21
Received welfare benefits, past 12 mo.	1.94	3.35
Ever filed bankruptcy	1.97	1.71
Ever arrested	2.00	3.15
Ever incarcerated	4.38	2.34
Ever divorced	2.29	1.38

Source: National Opinion Research Center, Gemini Research, The Lewin Group and Christiansen/Cummings Associates, *Gambling Impact and Behavior Study: Report to the National Gambling Impact Study Commission*, www.norc.uchicago.edu, downloaded April 1, 1999, Table 21, p. 58.

Both pathological and problem gamblers are clearly more likely to have had these adverse, costly experiences than low-risk gamblers. The most striking difference is involvement with the criminal justice system. Compared with low-risk gamblers, pathological gamblers are 4.38 times more likely to have been incarcerated, and problem gamblers are 3.15 times more likely to have been arrested. As one would expect given the difference in the severity of their gambling problems, the problem gamblers have a lower odds ratio than the pathological gamblers, with two interesting exceptions. Relative to the low-risk gamblers, problem gamblers are more likely than pathological gamblers to ever have been arrested, a difference for which there is no ready explanation. In addition, pathological gamblers are less likely than problem gamblers to have received welfare benefits during the past 12 months. One possibility here is that the pathological gamblers may have exhausted their eligibility for benefits by virtue of prior claims, resulting in a lower level of welfare benefit eligibility and use during the past year.

In the NORC study, an effort also was made to estimate the total economic costs of problem and pathological gambling. The results of this estimate for different kinds of costs are presented in Table 5.2.

TABLE 5.2
THE ECONOMIC COSTS OF PROBLEM AND
PATHOLOGICAL GAMBLING, PER GAMBLER

Type of cost	Who pays?	Problem		Pathological	
		Lifetime	Past year	Lifetime	Past year
Job loss	Employer	n.e.	$200	n.e.	$ 320
Unemployment benefits	Government	n.e.	65	n.e.	85
Welfare benefits	Government	n.e.	90	n.e.	60
Bankruptcy	Creditors	1,550	n.e.	3,300	n.e.
Arrests	Government	960	n.e.	1,250	n.e.
Corrections	Government	670	n.e.	1,700	n.e.
Divorce	Gambler/ spouse	1,950	n.e.	4,300	n.e.
Poor health	Health insurance	n.e.	0	n.e.	700
Poor mental health	Health insurance	n.e.	360	n.e.	330
Gambling treatment	Government	0	0	n.e.	30
TOTAL COSTS		$5,130	715	$10,550	$1,195

Source: National Opinion Research Center, Gemini Research, The Lewin Group and Christiansen/ Cummings Associates: *Gambling Impact and Behavior Study: Report to the National Gambling Impact Study Commission,* www.norc.uchicago.edu, downloaded April 1, 1999, Table 19, p. 52.
NOTE: n.e., means that it was not possible to estimate these costs.

The total *lifetime* costs per problem and pathological gambler are estimated to be $5,130 and $10,550, respectively. Using the NORC study's findings on the prevalence of pathological gambling, this translates into an aggregate lifetime cost of $4 billion for problem gamblers and $28 billion for pathological gamblers. If we assume that the average duration of problem and pathological gambling is about 50 years, these lifetime costs would work out to an *annual* cost of approximately $1 billion (in current dollars) (National Opinion Research Center et al., 1999:53).

In addition to this national survey, studies have been conducted in several states to identify the costs associated with problem gambling. In Louisiana, a study estimated the annual cost for each severe problem gambler at just less than $11,000, a figure considerably higher than the estimate from the NORC study, probably because of the inclusion of more cost items. The costs included hours lost from work by those unemployed, unemployment compensation, lost productivity because of unemployment, welfare costs, treatment costs, bad debts, thefts, civil court costs, and criminal court costs (including the cost of arrests, trials, probation, and incarceration) (Ryan and Speyrer, 1999). Similarly, a Wisconsin study concluded that the *annual* costs associated with each serious problem gambler were just less than $9,500. Here too, the costs included were both different and more comprehensive compared with the national, NORC, study. They included wages lost because of time spent gambling, unemployment compensation, income foregone because of unemployment, reduced productivity, bad debts, civil court costs, criminal justice system costs, treatment for problem gambling, and welfare costs (Thompson et al., 1996).

SUMMARY

The "costs" of problem gambling include monetary costs that can, with difficulty, be measured and "psychic" or psychological costs that are virtually impossible to measure. Costs to families, financial institutions, the criminal justice and human services systems, and employers have been described and documented where appropriate information exists.

The most recent and best national estimate is that, for those costs that can be measured and quantified, the total lifetime social costs per problem and pathological gambler are estimated to be $5,130 and

$10,550, respectively. Additional estimates indicate that pathological and problem gamblers generate an annual social cost of approximately $1 billion.

REFERENCES

Ahrons, S.J.: *A Comparison of the Family Environments and Psychological Distress of Married Pathological Gamblers, Alcoholics, Psychiatric Patients and Their Spouses with Normal Controls.* Unpublished Doctoral Dissertation, College Park: University of Maryland, 1989.

Ciarrocchi, Joseph W., and Hohnmann, Ann: The family environment of married male pathological gamblers, alcoholics, and dually addicted gamblers. *Journal of Gambling Behavior, 5*:283-291, 1989.

Epstein, Eileen A.: F*amily Functioning in the Families of Compulsive Gamblers.* Unpublished Doctoral Dissertation, New York, New York University, 1992.

Jacobs, Durand F.: Illegal and undocumented: A review of teenage gamblers in America. In Shaffer, Howard J., Stein, Sharon, Gambino, Blase, and Cummings, Thomas N. (Eds): *Compulsive Gambling: Theory, Research, and Practice,* Lexington, MA: Lexington Books, pp. 249 292, 1998.

Jacobs, Durand F., Marston, Albert R., Singer, Robert D., Widaman, Keith, Little, Todd, and Veizades, Jeannette. Children of problem gamblers. Journal of Gambling Behavior, 5: 261-268, 1989b.

Ladouceur, Robert, Boivert, Jean-Marie, Pepin, Michel, Loranger, Michel, and Sylvain, Caroline. Social cost of compulsive gambling. *Journal of Gambling Studies, 10*:399-409, 1994.

Lesieur, Henry R.: Measuring the costs of pathological gambling. Paper presented at the Eleventh Annual Conference on Problem Gambling, New Orleans, August, 1997.

Lesieur, Henry R., and Anderson, Christopher W.: *Results of a Survey of Gamblers Anonymous Members in Illinois.* Park Ridge, IL, Illinois Council on Problem and Compulsive Gambling, 1995.

Lesieur, Henry R. and Rothschild, J.: Children of gamblers anonymous members. *Journal of Gambling Behavior, 5*:269-282, 1989.

Lorenz, Valerie, 1981. Differences found among catholic, protestant, and jewish families of pathological gamblers. Paper presented at the Fifth National Conference on Gambling and Risk Taking, Reno, 1981.

Lorenz, Valerie, and Shuttlesworth, D. E.: The impact of pathological gambling on the spouse of the gambler. *Journal of Community Psychology, 11*:67-74, 1983.

Meyer, Gerhard, Fabian, Thomas, and Peter, Wolfgang: The social costs of pathological gambling. Paper presented at the First European Conference on Gambling Studies and Policy Issues, St John's College, Cambridge, United Kingdom, August, 1995.

National Opinion Research Center, Gemini Research, The Lewin Group, and Christiansen/ Cummings Associates: *Gambling Impact and Behavior Study: Report to the National Gambling Impact Study Commission.* www.norc.uchicago.edu, downloaded April 1, 1999.

Phillips, David P., Welty, Ward R, and Smith, Marisa A.: Elevated   suicide levels associated with legalized gambling. *Suicide and Life-Threatening Behavior, 27:*373-378, 1997.

Ryan, Timothy P., and Speyrer, Janet F.: *Gambling in Louisiana, A Benefit/Cost Analysis.* Shreveport, LA: Louisiana State University Medical Center, April, 1999.

Thompson, William N., Gazel, Ricardo, and Rickman, Dan: *The Social Costs of Gambling in Wisconsin.* Thiensville, Wisconsin Policy Research Institute, 9, No. 6, July, 1996.

Walker, Donald M., and Barnett, A.H.: The social costs of gambling: An economic perspective. *Journal of Gambling Studies, 15:*179-212, 1999.

Chapter 6

OBSTACLES AND PATHWAYS TO
TREATMENT FOR PROBLEM GAMBLING

It has been estimated that in the United States only about 3 percent of all pathological and problem gamblers actually seek help (Volberg, 1998). In an Indiana study, 2.8 percent of pathological gamblers sought inpatient treatment (Westphal et al., 1998). A study of British casino gamblers found that 4 percent of problem gamblers and 10 percent of "severe" problem gamblers had sought treatment (Fisher, 2000). In a study done in Alberta, Canada, 42 people who scored as problem or pathological gamblers on the South Oaks Gambling Screen were asked whether they had ever sought treatment in the form of either going to a counseling professional or to a meeting of a self-help group (e.g., Gamblers Anonymous). Only two respondents (4.8 percent)indicated that they had done so (Hodgins et al., 1999).

The ease with which problem gambling can be concealed and denied contributes to this extremely low rate of help-seeking on the part of problem gamblers. A number of other factors also contribute to this low rate of help-seeking.

OBSTACLES TO TREATMENT

Several factors that constitute obstacles to seeking treatment for problem gambling. This section provides a review and discussion of them.

Fear of Failure, Fear of Success

Problem gamblers' lives are filled with failures. They have failed to live up to their self-conception as smart, savvy gamblers. They may also have failed to get help from counselors or Gamblers Anonymous, and they have failed at efforts to control or cut back on their gambling. The very idea of getting help for a gambling problem is often viewed with a great deal of ambivalence and even as a threat. They may fear that treatment will not work and will turn out to be just another failure. At the same time, they may fear that, if treatment is successful, they may have to give up (in effect, "lose") what could well be the most meaningful, exciting, or comforting activity in their lives (Taber, 1985). Moreover, for problem gamblers, giving up gambling means leaving the world of fantasy to which they have escaped and confronting the problems and realities associated with everyday living in the "real world."

Denial

Denial has already been discussed in Chapter 2, but it is of special importance for the topic of treatment. For problem gamblers, denial is a major obstacle to getting help. Once gambling becomes the main activity in a person's life, giving it up may mean giving up one of the few things in life that has any meaning. Seeking help also means confronting the fact that one's fantasies about big wins are nothing more than fantasies. Counselors experienced in treating both problem gamblers and alcoholics routinely stress that denial is much stronger among the former. One of the main reasons for this is the fact that, as already pointed out, problem gambling is so easy to conceal and so difficult to detect.

With problem gamblers, denial is enhanced, because they can have "good days" when they win money and all their problems seem to be solved. Unlike the alcoholic, who rarely has what could be called a "good drunk," an afternoon of good fortune at a racetrack or a winning streak at a blackjack or craps table can bring (at least temporary) order into a chaotic life. When this happens, it becomes very easy for the problem gambler to say something like, "I don't have a problem with gambling, my problem was that I wasn't winning. Now everything's going to be OK." Under these circumstances, seeking help gets pushed out of the picture. When the inevitable losing streak resumes, problem gamblers expect the next "good day" to occur at any time, and getting help is further postponed.

Morality Issues

Gambling has been a moral issue throughout American history. Religious opposition to and condemnation of gambling were very evident during the Colonial era and the early nineteenth century (Findlay, 1986; Pavalko, 2000a). In contemporary American society, a minority of people, less than 10 percent, view gambling as a moral evil. However, there is still a tendency to view people who get into serious trouble with gambling as "bad" and "weak," as well as stupid and irresponsible.

The perception of gamblers who get into serious financial, family, and legal trouble because of their gambling as immoral people with flawed characters can be an important obstacle to treatment. This would be particularly important if the problem gambler sees himself or herself this way, and some do. Even if the problem gambler does not have this self-perception, she or he may believe that, if the problem is admitted, others, including counselors, may take this perspective. Simply the belief that one may be seen as an immoral person who has put personal gratification ahead of family and other responsibilities can be a powerful deterrent to seeking treatment.

Embarrassment

Admitting that one needs help for a gambling problem can be very embarrassing. The personality characteristics of many problem gamblers, such as arrogance, narcissism, and extroversion, as well as the belief that one can "beat the odds," are inconsistent with being willing to admit that one needs help. The bravado associated with being a "winner" leads problem gamblers to continue gambling to maintain the image (to themselves and others) that they are winners. To say that one is a "loser" and needs help is extremely difficult.

Although the obstacles to treatment discussed here apply to all problem gamblers, older problem gamblers may have special concerns about seeking treatment. Embarrassment and resentment may be especially intense among older people. Resentment in particular is an understandable response when anyone questions how they are spending their money. Having spent one's life working hard and saving, many older people believe that they have earned the right to spend their time and money as they please. If family members (particularly children) try to intervene and persuade an older problem gambler to see a counselor or go to a Gamblers Anonymous meeting, resentment may reach the point where relationships are seriously threatened. In this situation, it is not uncommon for older people to accuse those making suggestions of only being concerned with possible loss of future inheritances (see Pavalko, 2000b; 2001).

Absence of Referral Mechanisms

Compared with chemical dependence, referral mechanisms for problem gambling are much less well developed. As we have already seen, referral for problem gambling counseling by mental health professionals does not occur routinely. There are no legally mandated counseling programs for problem gambling as there are for many situations involving chemical addiction. Problem gambling isn't a crime, unlike illegal drug possession and use, public drunkenness, or drunk driving. Drug law violators may have treatment forced on them. Some states and the federal government may commit people to treatment programs for alcohol and other drug addiction. In prisons, participation in drug treatment programs may be mandated, and enrollment in treatment programs may be a condition of probation or parole (Akers, 1992:165). None of these things happen in the case of problem gambling. Consequently, the legal and criminal justice systems do not serve as meaningful referral mechanisms.

Financial Concerns

By the time most problem gamblers seek treatment, they have financially hit "rock bottom." Besides not having any money, they are heavily in debt. Their financial resources are not only nonexistent, they are "negative." Consequently, the cost of treatment can be a major barrier to seeking treatment. Although publicly funded programs exist, they are not readily available throughout the United States and, where they exist, problem gamblers may not be aware of them despite efforts to publicize them. Because health insurance policies do not usually cover problem gambling treatment, problem gamblers ready for some kind of help may not seek it.

How Problem Gamblers Explain Their Gambling

One of the things that is difficult to understand about problem gamblers is why, in the face of mounting and extreme financial, family, work, legal, and other difficulties, they continue gambling and postpone or avoid getting help. Richard Rosenthal and Loreen Rugle (1994), both of whom have a great deal of experience treating problem gamblers, have provided some answers to this question by looking at what gambling means to problem gamblers and the kinds of "explanations" they offer for why they gamble.

Rosenthal and Rugle argue that problem gamblers need and desire spectacular success as a way of demonstrating their worth to themselves and others. Gambling, especially if they are successful at it also is a way of gaining approval from others. Anger and rebellion are also involved. When problem gamblers are angry at someone, such as a spouse, gambling may be seen as a way of punishing the other person, often with the expectation that the other person will be humiliated by the gambler's winnings. Problem gamblers may also use gambling to express rebellious, antiauthority feelings. In effect, the act of gambling comes to symbolize nonconformity and affirms one's rejection of conventional norms.

For the problem gambler, gambling is also a way of gaining freedom and independence from others. What seems to be involved here is the belief that if one could just win enough to quit one's job or get a divorce, one could put an end to being subject to the whims and demands of others. Rosenthal and Rugle also argue that gamblers often confuse potential financial independence with emotional independence from others.

For many problem gamblers, gambling may also be a way of gaining social acceptance. Many problem gamblers report "feeling good" when they get "perks" (free drinks, complimentary meals, or show tickets) when gambling in casinos or when a blackjack or craps dealer remembers their name. A sense of kinship with other gamblers, bookies, casino or track personnel is often experienced in a way that makes problem gamblers feel "included" and part of something.

Gambling is also clearly a way of escaping painful or intolerable feelings. Rosenthal and Rugle describe this as a kind of "self-medication." What this means is that gambling may function as an antidepressant or to prolong and intensify the manic phase of bipolar (manic/depressive) disorder (Rosenthal and Rugle, 1994:30).

A final meaning that gambling may have for problem gamblers has to do with competitiveness. Rosenthal and Rugle point out that problem gamblers are very competitive. Competitiveness may be the result of trying to impress and please parents, a spouse, or others. It can develop into a trait expressed in many different situations—work, school, etc. For some people, gambling becomes a competitive activity in which losing is not only unacceptable but actually unthinkable, and the potential for persisting at gambling and "chasing one's losses" becomes enormous.

Clearly, with gambling having all these meanings and serving a variety of functions, it makes sense that people in trouble with gambling would be reluctant to seek help that might lead to having to give up gambling. With so much at stake, these meanings and functions serve as an additional obstacle to seeking treatment.

PATHWAYS TO TREATMENT

How do people get into treatment for a gambling addiction? The decision to seek help usually occurs when something dramatic happens, there is no other option, and they are coerced or blackmailed into getting help. A spouse or partner may leave or threaten to leave or file for divorce. A lawyer representing a person arrested for a gambling-related crime may get the client into treatment in an effort to convince a judge or jury that the person has acknowledged his or her gambling problem and is doing something about it. Having embezzled money from an employer or clients, seeking help may be offered as an alternative to filing criminal charges. A bank or loan company may threaten to foreclose. Or, a failed suicide attempt may dramatize the scope of the problem and prompt a search for help.

Although problem gamblers should be referred to a qualified problem gambling counselor, other counselors and people dealing with problem gamblers in many roles may encounter people with a gambling problem and be in a position to provide assistance, information, and referral. Those working in human service agencies that deal with family, alcohol, or other drug problems could serve a screening and referral function, but, as already has been noted, knowledge about problem gambling among human service agency personnel is minimal. The clergy are another potential source of referrals, as are physicians and people working in both private and public financial counseling organizations. Unfortunately, we have very little systematic data about how frequently referrals by any of these sources occur.

Another source of referral is the "state councils" on problem gambling. Most of these councils operate toll-free telephone "helplines" that people in trouble with their gambling can call for information about problem gambling and information on how to find qualified counselors and Gamblers Anonymous meetings near where they live. Because calls to these helplines are anonymous, it is impossible to follow up and know what proportion of people who call actually go to a counselor or a Gamblers Anonymous meeting. Nevertheless, the volume of such calls is significant. For illustrative purposes, Table 6.1 presents data on phone calls to the helplines of six state councils. The number of calls per day ranges from 3.4 in Connecticut to 15.2 in Oregon. All the councils included in Table 6.1 report that the number of calls has increased significantly over the past several years.

With 35 state councils on problem gambling operating such helplines, they serve as an important source of information and potential referral for the treatment of problem gambling. Rugle (1999) reports that, nationwide, between 60 and 70 percent of callers are seeking help for themselves, whereas 30 to 40 percent are other people (spouse, other family member, friend, counselor, employer) calling about a problem gambler.

When problem gamblers do seek help, appropriate treatment by qualified problem gambling counselors may not be readily available. Results from a gambling prevalence study in Indiana illustrate this. The study concluded that 0.8 percent of Indiana's adults (34,493 people) were pathological gamblers and that 965 sought inpatient treatment for their gambling problem. However, during 1997 and 1998 (the time period of the study) only 31 and 99 people, respectively, were actually enrolled in inpatient treatment programs specifically designed to treat people with gambling problems (Westphal et al.,

1998). This suggests that most problem gamblers who sought treatment either were not being treated or were being treated in programs that probably were not designed to deal with their gambling problem.

TABLE 6.1
PHONE CALLS TO SELECTED STATE COUNCIL HELPLINES

State	Year	Number of calls per year	Number of calls per day
Connecticut	1998	1,240	3.4
Iowa	1998	3,522	9.6
Indiana	1998	1,507	4.1
New York	2000	1,453*	8.0
Oregon	1998	2,784*	15.2
Wisconsin	2000	5,052	14.8

* During a six month period.
Sources: Rugle, Loreen: The treatment of pathological gambling. Indianapolis, Indiana University Center for Urban Policy and the Environment, 1999; Wisconsin Council on Problem Gambling: Helpline statistics, 1996, 1997, 1998, 1999 comparison. Green Bay, Wisconsin Council on Problem Gambling, January, 2001; and *Council News*, New York Council on Problem Gambling, Albany, Summer, 2000.

SUMMARY

Problem gamblers are very reluctant to admit they have a problem and seek help. Getting into treatment may be seen as losing the only thing (gambling) that provides meaning to their lives. They deny that they have a problem for as long as they can; they dread being seen by others as a bad, immoral, or irresponsible persons; and they may be embarrassed to admit that they have gotten into financial and other difficulties because of their gambling.

The absence of established referral mechanisms within the criminal justice and human service systems also results in a low rate of help-seeking on the part of problem gamblers. Problem gamblers usually do not seek help until they face some crisis that they simply cannot deal with otherwise. This may be the threatened or actual departure of a spouse or partner, loss of a job, arrest and impending legal action, no possibility of borrowing additional money to gamble with or pay off gambling debts, or an unsuccessful suicide attempt.

REFERENCES

Akers, Ronald L.: *Drugs, Alcohol, and Society: Social Structure, Process, and Policy.* Belmont, CA: Wadsworth, 1922.

Findlay, John M.: *People of Chance: Gambling in American Society From Jamestown to Las Vegas.* New York: Oxford University Press, 1986.

Fisher, Susan: Measuring the prevalence of sector-specific problem gambling: A study of casino patrons. *Journal of Gambling Studies,* 25-51, 2000.

Hodgins, David C., Wynne, Harold, and Makarchuk, Karyn: Pathways to recovery from gambling problems: Follow-up from a general population survey. *Journal of Gambling Studies, 15:*93-104, 1999.

Pavalko, Ronald M.: *Risky Business: America's Fascination with Gambling.* Belmont, CA: Wadsworth, 2000a.

Pavalko, Ronald M.: Problem gambling among older adults. *Focus on geriatric care and rehabilitation, 14:* October, 2000b.

Pavalko, Ronald M.: Problem gambling among older people. In Gurnack, Anne M., Atkinson, Roland, and Osgood, Nancy (Eds).: *Treating Alcohol and Drug Abuse in the Elderly,* New York: Springer Publications, 2001.

Rosenthal, Richard J., and Rugle, Loreen J.: A Psychodynamic approach to the treatment of pathological gambling: Part I: Achieving abstinence. *Journal of Gambling Studies, 10:*21-42, 1994.

Rugle, Loreen: *The treatment of pathological gambling.* Indianapolis, Indiana Univerity Center for Urban Policy and the Environment, 1999.

Taber, Julian I.: Pathological gambling: The initial screening interview. *Journal of Gambling Behavior, 1:*23-34, 1985.

Volberg, Rachel A.: *Gambling and Problem Gambling in Oregon: A Report to the Oregon Gambling Addiction Treatment Foundation.* Northampton, MA: Gemini Research, 1998.

Westphal, J.R., Rush, J.A., and Stevens, L.: *Problem and Pathological Gambling Behaviors Within Specific Populations in the State of Indiana.* Shreveport: LA, Louisiana State University Medical Center, 1998.

Chapter 7

TREATING PROBLEM GAMBLING

ISSUES IN THE TREATMENT OF PROBLEM GAMBLING

Several major, unresolved issues exist in the treatment of problem gambling. One of these is what the goal of treatment should be. Some counselors see a complete cessation of gambling as the goal, in effect replacing gambling with "not gambling" as the focal point of the gambler's life. Others see this as a crucial first step but see the identification and treatment of the underlying problems that led to problem gambling as the real goal. Counselors who take the latter position will take a more "holistic" approach and emphasize dealing with the motivations for gambling, interpersonal problems to which gambling is related, and the psychodynamics of gambling behavior.

A related and unresolved issue is whether total abstinence from gambling is essential for successful treatment. Most problem gambling counselors and Gamblers Anonymous take the position that abstinence is essential. However, the possibility that a problem gambler could learn to become a "controlled gambler" has been raised by more than a few researchers (Dickerson, 1984; Rosecrance, 1988). John Rosecrance, a critic of the conventional "medical model" interpretation of problem gambling, has argued that, for many problem gamblers, abstinence may be an unrealistic (and unnecessary) goal (Rosecrance, 1988). Other researchers, both sociologists and psychologists, have also taken the position that the "loss of control" implied by the terms "compulsive" and "pathological" gambling is overstated and misplaced. Research on gamblers in natural settings and experiments designed to teach problem gamblers to gamble in a controlled way suggest that there may well be options to the goal of total abstinence in treating problem gambling (Dickerson, 1984; Dickerson et al., 1979; Hayano, 1982; Oldman, 1978; Rankin, 1982; Scott, 1968). This issue is similar to the debate that has developed regarding whether or not it is possible for alcoholics to become "controlled drinkers" (Fingarette, 1988).

TREATMENT STRATEGIES

Logically, the solution to any problem should be based on an understanding of its cause. Herein lies a major difficulty in the treatment of problem gambling. Its cause is not clearly understood, and there are, in all likelihood, multiple causes. Consequently, it is not surprising that no single treatment approach has emerged. No one, single technique for treating problem gambling that most counselors use or would agree on exists, except that virtually all counselors agree that, to be effective, individual counseling needs to be combined with participation in Gamblers Anonymous. Typically, most counselors take a pragmatic approach, using what works and avoiding being locked in to one single strategy.

Treating problem gambling basically involves dramatically changing the problem gambler's lifestyle, behavior, and the irrational, fantasy-based way in which the person has come to think about gambling. For many problem gamblers, gambling is a symptom of an underlying problem that they have been trying to avoid dealing with. To be effective, treatment may have to deal with those problems, as well as the gambling per se, and develop new problem-solving skills.

A first step in treatment often is simply educating the person about the nature of the disorder. Problem gamblers tend to be confused and bewildered. They see other people gambling without adverse consequences and cannot understand why they are unable do so. Educating them about problem gambling at least gives their difficulties a name. That alone can provide some reassurance that help is possible. It may also provide them with them the sense that they are not alone, that others have the same problem.

Problem gamblers' finances are usually in a state of absolute chaos. Besides owing money to friends and relatives, credit card issuers, finance companies, loan sharks, bookies, and casinos, they frequently have not bothered to file federal and state income tax returns for some time. They may also be facing foreclosure on home or business mortgages. Assistance from a lawyer or credit counselor may be needed to bring some semblance of order into the problem gambler's financial and related legal difficulties. Legal help may also be needed to deal with outstanding or imminent criminal charges resulting from bad checks, forgery, embezzlement, tax fraud, or insurance fraud.

It is also essential to develop a household budget that may include putting the problem gambler on an allowance, something that the problem gambler can be expected to object to very strongly. Also essential is developing a "restitution plan" for paying back all the people and organizations from which money has been borrowed. One of the benefits of this is to force confrontation of the scope of the financial problem and the impact that gambling has had on others.

If employed, it is likely that the problem gambler's job is in jeopardy because of absenteeism, tardiness, and less than conscientious work performance. If this is the case, informing the employer of the nature of the employee's problem and the treatment plan is necessary. In the case of older, retired people who are not employed, it would not be necessary to be concerned about this.

If chemical addiction is present, treatment will need to deal with this problem too. However, it is not appropriate to deal with problem gamblers (dually addicted or not) by getting them only into counseling or self-help groups designed to deal only with chemical addiction.

Some "key components" of successful treatment efforts have been identified by Blaszczynski and Silove (1995). They reviewed more than a dozen different therapies and identified nine common elements of successful treatment. These are presented in Table 7.1.

Following these guidelines is no assurance of success. Relapse is very high among problem gamblers. They do, however, represent a core of conditions that will maximize the likelihood of success. One of the therapist's responsibilities is to make sure that these conditions are being met.

TABLE 7.1
KEY COMPONENTS OF SUCCESSFUL TREATMENT

1. To avoid the risk of relapse, the problem gambler should avoid exposure to gambling cues and situations and involvement with other gamblers.

2. Stress management techniques need to be used to lower arousal and anxiety and serve as a more appropriate way of coping than gambling.

3. If "dysphoric mood" (especially depression) is experienced, antidepressants may need to be prescribed by a physician.

4. Illogical and erroneous beliefs, attitudes, and expectations regarding gambling need to be challenged and corrected with an emphasis placed on preventing relapse.

5. Marriage/family counseling may be needed to reestablish trust between partners.

6. Budgeting skills and acceptance of financial responsibility need to be developed with a concern for meeting financial obligations without gambling.

7. Developing nongambling leisure activities ia essential.

8. If present, addiction to alcohol or other drugs needs to be addressed.

9. Attending Gamblers Anonymous meetings and attending GamAnon meetings by the spouse is essential.

Source: Adapted from Blaszczynski, Alex, and Silove, Derrick: Cognitive and behavioral therapies for pathological gambling. *Journal of Gambling Studies, 11*:195-220, 1995.

BEHAVIORAL AND COGNITIVE MODELS OF TREATMENT

Models are basically sets of interconnected ideas, assumptions, principles, and guidelines used to try to understand and deal with some phenomenon. It is useful to think about ways of dealing with problem gambling as constituting "treatment models."

Contemporary treatment strategies rely primarily on two models–behavioral and cognitive. The goal of the discussion that follows is to illustrate these models rather than present a detailed discussion of their nuances. However, before explaining these models, it is essential to note two additional approaches to treating problem gambling: psychoanalysis and pharmacology (treatment with drugs).

Psychoanalysis is important because of its historical significance. The earliest reports of identifying and treating problem gambling were done by psychoanalysis (see Pavalko, 2000 and Rosenthal, 1987 for a review of this work). Sigmund Freud, for example, identified similarities between alcohol, other drug, and gambling addiction. Psychoanalysis is not favored as a treatment for problem gambling by contemporary counselors. In addition to being pessimistic about the prospects for recovery, psychoanalysis regards gambling as an attempt to resolve conflicts with authority figures, an issue that, in the opinion of counselors, does not seem to be part of the experiences of problem gamblers (see McCown and Chamberlain, 2000 for a discussion of these issues).

There have been and continue to be efforts to treat problem gamblers with a variety of drugs, including antidepressants and serotonin reuptake inhibitors (Hollander et al., 1998; Lesieur, 1998). Such *pharmacological treatment* is highly experimental, and at a relatively early stage, and not widely used among treatment professionals.

Behavioral Treatment

As the term implies, behavioral treatment focuses on changing, or modifying, the behavior of the problem gambler. It is based largely on the principles of learning theory initially formulated and developed by B.F. Skinner (1953). The key assumption in this model is that gambling is a learned (maladaptive) behavior that can be unlearned using techniques based on learning theory (Blaszczynski and Silove, 1995). As a form of treatment, the focus is on day-to-day behavior (the "one day at a time" approach), with little attention given to the psychodynamics involved in producing the original, problematic gambling behavior.

An example of behavioral treatment is "aversion therapy," which seeks to produce an adverse or negative reaction to the activity or behavior that the therapist is trying to change (i.e., gambling). The strategy is to pair gambling with some negative stimulus such as nausea, extreme cold, or electric shock (McCown and Chamberlain, 2000). "Aversive imagery" is a variant on this strategy. Here, the problem gambler imagines gambling situations and learns to connect them with something negative and unpleasant. McCown and Chamberlain (2000:138) report a case in which a problem gambler learned to stop thinking about gambling. He would shout out loud "Stop, goddam it!" every time he began to think about gambling. This "thought-stopping" process led to a dramatic cessation of his gambling behavior.

In a case the author is familiar with, a problem gambler in his 50s drove past a casino five days a week on his way to and from work. He found it increasingly difficult to do so without stopping at the casino to play blackjack. ("The car just takes the off-ramp to the casino all by itself!") By the time he sought help, he was stopping more often than not, showing up late for work, missing work altogether, not coming home after work, and sometimes gambling from the time he got off work until it was time to go to work the next day. In addition, he exhibited most of the classic symptoms of a problem gambler (he scored 13 on the South Oaks Gambling Screen). One of the first things that was done was to devise a new route for him to take to and from work that did not involve driving past the casino. Although this added a few minutes to his commute, it altered his behavior so that the connection between the drive to work and gambling was changed. This by no means solved his gambling problem, but it set in motion a change in behavior on which other changes could be built.

The behavioral model does have its critics (Schewan and Brown, 1993; Sharpe and Tarrier, 1993) who argue that behavioral assumptions alone cannot explain problem gambling. Learning theory, on which the behavioral model is based, would lead us to expect persistent gambling to continue only if it was "positively reinforcing." Because problem gambling, virtually by definition, involves serious negative personal, family, legal, and other problems, one would not expect problem gamblers to continue gambling in the face of all the painful, negative experiences they have, but they nevertheless continue to do so.

This criticism implies that behavioral approaches to the treatment of problem gambling alone will not suffice, and they need to be used in conjunction with techniques based on the cognitive model. Many therapists have accepted this view, and, consequently, we find treatment programs based on what has come to be known as a "cognitive-behavioral model."

Cognitive Treatment

Although treatment techniques based on the behavioral model emphasize changing immediate behavior, the cognitive approach stresses changing the thinking of the problem gambler. The strategy here is to challenge and change many of the incorrect or irrational beliefs of problem gamblers and demonstrate that those beliefs lead to irrational (gambling) behavior (Beck et al., 1979; Wessler, 1993). There are many such beliefs, some of which are held by non-problem gamblers as well as problem gamblers.

One of the most basic and common beliefs of problem gamblers is that there is a pattern to outcomes that are completely random. For example, a slot machine player may believe that a symbol that has not come up for a long time is "due" to come up, or one that has come up frequently is not going to come up for a long time. A lottery player notices that the number 12 hasn't been drawn for the past two weeks, so it must be due. The blackjack player loses 10 hands in a row and concludes that the next hand *has* to be a winner. All these conclusions are wrong, because the outcomes involved are all the result of a completely random process. McCown and Chamberlain (2000:143) report using an interesting technique for addressing this cognitive distortion. After using a computer to generate a long sequence of random numbers, they have problem gamblers look at the list and ask them to identify the pattern (which of course does not exist). Most problem gamblers, however, will find a pattern. When the nature of the sequence of numbers is explained, many problem gamblers will challenge the nonexistence of a pattern. Showing them the statement "Random Number Generator" in the computer program may be necessary, but even that may not always succeed in changing their beliefs.

Another example of irrational thinking involves a betting "system" used by many gamblers (problem and nonproblem alike) and one that actually is recommended by some "experts" who write advice books for gamblers. It is the system of *doubling any bet after a loss*. A basic feature of any casino game is "the more and the longer you bet, the more you lose." In other words, it takes time for the laws of probability and the house advantage built into the games to catch up with the gambler. This "system" constitutes a belief that leads to behavior that is contrary to the structure of the games and encourages what is essentially the behavior we call "chasing" one's losses. In a similar process, most gamblers will decrease their bet after a loss (i.e., in the face of losses, they become more conservative), but problem gamblers will do the opposite; when they lose, they will increase their bet, believing that the next bet is a "sure thing" or that they are due to win. The task of treatment is to point out and demonstrate the irrationality of this kind of thinking. The very idea of a "sure thing" or a "hunch" is completely contradictory to the very rational principles (i.e., the laws of probability) that govern how gambling games operate.

In addition, there are other commonly held beliefs of problem gamblers that treatment may need to address. These include the belief that one has more control over events than actually exists and the belief that one has more skill (e.g., at picking a winning horse or team) than one really has. Various superstitions, a belief that one is exceptionally "lucky," and the belief that one has special attributes that provide an "edge" over other players (or a casino or racetrack), are additional beliefs that may need to be challenged, relinquished, or changed.

These examples of how the behavioral and cognitive models bear upon treatment apply to both individual and group therapy and inpatient and outpatient treatment. The principles of the behavioral and cognitive models are not used alone. They usually are used in conjunction with referral to Gamblers Anonymous.

RELAPSE

Regardless of the primary approach used or the balance between behavioral and cognitive strategies, *relapse* (i.e., returning to gambling) is a serious concern in treatment. Problem gamblers in treatment need to be alerted to the fact that relapse can occur, but if it does occur, it does not mean that treatment has been a failure. Relapses are almost inevitable. It is essential to make clear to the problem gambler that, when they occur, they must be admitted, confronted, and treatment must be resumed. Problem gamblers may try to use a relapse as a reason to give up on treatment altogether. Some may even intentionally relapse as a way of "proving" to themselves and the therapist that treatment is futile. Discussion of relapse and what needs to happen after a relapse (i.e., returning to treatment) needs to be addressed early in the treatment process. The postrelapse resumption of treatment needs to include an examination of why it occurred, what triggered the gambling, and devising a way of avoiding those triggers in the future. In effect, relapse should be turned into a learning experience.

Once people have entered treatment, a number of things can occur that can trigger a relapse. Just about anything that upsets or frustrates people has relapse potential. Anger; stress; an argument with a spouse, partner, other family member, or friend; a bad day at work; money problems, etc., are all candidates for triggering a return to gambling. Especially early in the treatment process, many problem gamblers may still be toying with the idea that maybe they aren't really problem gamblers and maybe they could learn to be controlled gamblers. How does one find out for sure? By gambling, of course! When this happens, any sense of achievement and recovery that the problem gambler has been developing can be shattered. Problem gamblers with long periods of abstinence may believe that they are "cured" and can gamble in a limited, controlled way. Here too, the way to test this belief is by gambling. The situation is analogous to the recovering alcoholic who believes that he or she can handle one drink, which turns into a multiday binge. Relapses may be of relatively short duration, or the problem gambler may continue to gamble until "rock bottom" has been reached again. Problem gamblers with long periods of successful recovery indicate that, in retrospect, they could not stop until they hit bottom (perhaps several times) and experienced such extreme suffering and self-loathing that abstinence became the only option.

TREATING THE FAMILY

The treatment of problem gambling involves more than just the treatment of the gambler. It necessarily includes treating the problem gambler's spouse and children. In the case of older people, it may also mean including grandchildren. Typically, family members have treated the problem gambler's gambling as a "passing interest." They might at some point have been concerned that the gambling was excessive but denied its significance. If family members have confronted the gambler, they have probably been assured by the gambler that "its under control and nothing to be concerned about." Problem gamblers are very good at conning other people and convincing them that "there's no problem."

Family members are likely to be even more confused than the gambler about what has been going on. As with the gambler, education and information about the nature of problem gambling are needed.

The money management issues dealt with earlier clearly need to involve the spouse and often other immediate family members. Children, grandchildren, and other relatives may have inadvertently facilitated the problem gambler by providing loans, alibis, and other bailouts. They may feel responsible for contributing to the acceleration of the problem gambler's difficulties.

Family members in many cases have denied the existence of a problem for at least as long as the problem gambler has been denying it. They have been the victims of the problem gambler's lies and deceit. Frustration with and resentment of the problem gambler are likely to be intense, especially on the part of the spouse and children who have experienced material and emotional deprivations because of the gambler's behavior.

Spouses have typically engaged in a great deal of denial of a problem, explaining the gambler's behavior as a temporary problem. Frustration and resentment usually mount as unpaid bills pile up, creditors become more insistent about payment, and the inability of the gambler to control his or her gambling becomes more and more evident. Spouses may have been encouraged by the problem gambler to accompany him or her to a gambling venue, seen the problem gambler "in action" but not understood the problem gambler's behavior; one task of family treatment is to explain it to the nongambling spouse. Having lied and hidden the problem from friends and family members, spouses are likely to have become withdrawn from others to avoid embarrassment. They also may have considered divorce or separation as a way of dealing with their problems.

In some cases spouses become depressed to the point at which they become ineffective at work and as a parent. A vague sense of distress, confusion, and anxiety are common and, in extreme cases, so is impaired thinking and an inability to function in normal roles. As two counselors with experience in the treatment of problem gamblers and their families have put it, the spouse ". . . may feel helpless and hopeless, may be abusing substances (especially alcohol and pills), considering divorce, suffering from depression, and in the extreme, considering suicide" (Franklin and Thoms, 1989:138). Individual counseling for the spouse and marriage and family counseling for the entire family is needed in many cases. One study of the spouses of compulsive gamblers identified them as angry, depressed, isolated from the gambling spouse, guilty, suicidal, and experiencing a variety of stress-related physical symptoms including headaches, insomnia, and various aches and pains (Lorenz and Yaffee, 1989).

WHAT WORKS AND WHAT DOESN'T?
THE ASSESSMENT OF TREATMENT

The issue of how effective different kinds of treatment are is one of the most neglected topics in the area of problem gambling studies. A dearth of research exists on the topic, and the research that does exist is rather limited in scope.

An ideal evaluation of treatment programs would involve several steps. First, one would want a randomly selected group of problem gamblers entering treatment that were representative of all problem gamblers. Second, people would be assigned randomly to different kinds of treatment. In addition, one would want to have one randomly selected group of problem gamblers that received no treatment. Such a "control group" would be needed for comparison purposes to ensure that changes in the gambling behavior of the treatment groups was actually a result of the treatment. Finally, one would want to do follow-ups of the treatment (and control) groups to assess the permanence of any changes in their gambling behavior.

Given the characteristics of problem gamblers and the conditions under which they enter treatment, meeting the criteria just identified is a formidable task and one that probably cannot be met in reality. Getting representative, let alone random, samples of problem gamblers is virtually impossible, because treatment programs obviously deal only with people seeking treatment. As we already know, those who seek treatment are not representative of the universe of problem gamblers. Ethical dilemmas are also involved in assigning people who want and need treatment to a control group that receives no treatment.

A major, unresolved issue in evaluating the success of treatment is how success is defined. People may successfully complete treatment without necessarily changing their gambling behavior after treatment. Successful treatment may be defined in various ways including total abstinence from gambling, or "controlled gambling" in which there is a reduction in the frequency of gambling or the amount of money wagered or lost. If success is defined as abstinence, how long does one have to be abstinent before treatment is judged to have been successful? There is no consensus among those working in the field of gambling studies on what the time period should be. In the case of controlled gambling, no consensus exists on how long controlled gambling needs to be maintained before treatment is deemed successful. The research on treatment evaluation that does exist varies considerably in terms of the outcome that is measured and the time period involved.

The careers of problem gamblers often include cycles of abstinence followed by "relapses" (i.e., returning to gambling) and often periods of controlled gambling mixed in with the abstinence and uncontrolled gambling. In a hypothetical case in which a problem gambler completes treatment, is abstinent, relapses, becomes abstinent, engages in control gambling, relapses, becomes abstinent, etc., there is obviously a dilemma involved in judging the success or failure of treatment. Clearly, the judgment will depend on where in the cycle one observes the person.

Given the difficulties that result from the abstinence/controlled gambling/relapse cycle, one possibility would be to define success in terms of a reduction in the problems (family, work, legal, etc.) that the problem gambler had before treatment. If this approach were taken, one would then face the problem of deciding *how much of a reduction* in those problems had to occur to define treatment as successful.

A final issue that the evaluation of treatment needs to deal with is the kinds of expectations and desires both counselors and problem gamblers hold as treatment begins. If counselors or problem gamblers (or both) expect treatment to be successful, those expectations may influence the outcome (i.e., produce success). Similarly, if expectations of failure (or minimal success) are held, they may lead to the expected result. The issue involves a classic case of the *self-fulfilling prophecy*, in which the results obtained are shaped by peoples' expectations of what that result will be (McCown and Chamberlain, 2000). Although it is very unlikely that counselors would *desire* treatment to fail, it is not unrealistic to believe that some problem gamblers may not want it to succeed. As has already been pointed out, if treatment succeeds, the problem gambler has a great deal to lose and has to confront the issue of totally changing his or her life. Again, the self-fulfilling prophecy may confound the task of evaluating the success of treatment.

What the Research Shows

Most reports of *psychoanalytic* treatment involve single cases of people treated, making the evaluation of the effectiveness of psychoanalysis extremely difficult. Only one study of sufficient size exists to warrant being called an evaluation of this type of treatment. In the 1950s, Edmund Bergler reported that of 60 patients who entered psychodynamic therapy, 45 (75 percent) were "cured" of their gambling or "cured" of all their neurotic symptoms, including gambling (Bergler, 1957). However, it is unclear as to precisely how it was determined that people were "cured" and how Bergler's findings should be interpreted (Walker, 1993).

As indicated earlier, treating problem gamblers with drugs is still in the experimental stage. An early study reported positive results with lithium carbonate (Moskowitz, 1980). Clomipramine (Hollander et al., 1992), fluoximine (Saiz, 1992), and fluvoxamine (Hollander et al., 1998) have also been tried with moderate success. Given the extremely small sample size in these studies (ranging from 1 to 10 cases) the treatment of problem gamblers with drugs is not likely to become a widespread form of treatment in the foreseeable future.

Although some research has evaluated the effectiveness of strategies based on the *behavioral and cognitive* models, none of it meets the level of methodological rigor needed for such research discussed earlier. Consequently, the findings we have need to be viewed as suggestive rather than definitive.

Research supports the conclusion that treatment that includes participation in Gamblers Anonymous, relapse prevention, the development of coping and problem-solving skills, budgeting and financial restitution, and family involvement are effective in helping problem gamblers achieve and maintain abstinence for a period of time ranging from six months to one year (Rugle, 1999).

Blaszczynski and Silove (1995) reviewed twenty studies of the outcomes of treatment programs using a variety of techniques based on the behavioral model. The studies were done between 1970 and 1992. Most of these studies were based on very small numbers of cases (one to seven people). However, in nine of them, findings were based on between 10 and 124 cases. Using just these nine studies, it is possible to get an overall picture of how well behavioral treatments work. Although the studies evaluating treatment used different outcome measures, people who completed treatment can be classified as abstinent, engaged in controlled gambling (where the amount of time and money spent gambling is reduced), or engaging in uncontrolled gambling (i.e., gambling similar to that engaged in before treatment). The studies also differ in the time period between completion of treatment and the measurement of what kind of gambling, if any, people were engaged in; the time periods used ranged from six months to five years. These nine studies dealt with treatment programs in which a total of 466 people completed treatment. Only 272 (58.4) were actually located for the follow-up part of the research to identify what they were doing in terms of gambling. Of the 272 who were found, 60.3 percent were abstinent, 17.3 percent were engaging in controlled gambling, and 22.4 percent were uncontrolled gamblers. A serious problem with these studies is, of course, the large proportion (42 percent) of the treatment completers who were not located. Just how they are distributed in terms of abstinence, controlled, or uncontrolled gambling remains an unanswerable question.

Included in the nine outcome studies just summarized are two in which more detailed comments can help to illustrate treatment outcomes. An evaluation of a comprehensive residential, inpatient treatment program at the Brecksville, Ohio, Veterans Administration Hospital found that 56 percent of the patients completing the program did not gamble at all during the first six months after completion of the program, and 55 percent were abstinent after one year (Taber et al., 1987). A residential, inpatient treatment program at a private hospital was evaluated by Lesieur and Blume (1991). They found that 64 percent of the problem gamblers were abstinent for periods ranging from four to 16 months after completing treatment.

The review of treatment outcomes by Blaszczynski and Silove (1995) already discussed included a review of studies of treatment programs using strategies based on the *cognitive* as well as the behavioral model. Two of the six cognitive studies were based on just one case (i.e., one person completing treatment). However, in four studies the number of people completing a particular program ranges between 58 and 124; all were conducted between 1977 and 1992. The time period between completion of treatment and contact with those completing treatment varied from six months to two years. A total of 320 people completed treatment in these four programs. When the follow-up studies were done, 53.4 percent (171 people) of those completing treatment were located. Of these 171, 72 percent were abstinent, 8 percent were engaged in "reduced gambling with periodic abstinence," and 20 percent were gambling, but it is impossible to say whether they were gambling in a "controlled" or "uncontrolled" manner. As with the studies of treatment based on behavioral principles, the fact that 46.6 percent of those completing treatment could not be found in the follow-up suggests the need for cautious conclusions. Superficially, it seems that there is higher a rate of abstinence in programs based on cognitive compared with behavioral principles. Because, in the studies of programs using behavioral and cognitive treatments, there are differences in the research procedures, the time frames used, and the definition of outcomes, not too much should be made of the relatively higher rate of "success" (i.e., abstinence) for the cognitively based treatment programs. Clearly, both are effective in achieving abstinence, reduced gambling, and controlled gambling, and both have a place in treatment.

One of the largest and most comprehensive treatment evaluations that has been done was conducted in Minnesota; it has not been included in the summary of behaviorally and cognitively based programs discussed up to this point. Six treatment programs, operated by the Minnesota Department of Human Services, began operating in 1991. Payment for treatment includes a combination of state funding, insurance, and self-pay. One facility has residential, inpatient, treatment, whereas the others offer outpatient treatment. Treatment occurs in a group therapy format and incudes a wide range of techniques and strategies, including some based on the behavioral and cognitive models. Between September, 1991, and April, 1997, 880 problem gamblers entered the programs. Not everyone who entered these programs completed them. For example, in a typical year, treatment completion rates ranged between 29 and 87 percent. The evaluation of the programs indicated that treatment was valuable for most of people who completed the programs. At the time they completed the programs, 77 percent indicated that they were not gambling. Contacted at six months and one year after treatment, 55 percent said that they were not gambling. An additional 15 to 25 percent (depending on the particular program) indicated that they were gambling less than once per month. The follow-up of these people also found that they had less gambling debt, fewer financial problems, and fewer gambling friends compared with when they entered the programs (Rugle, 1999; Stinchfield and Winters, 1996).

SUMMARY

Two controversies exist regarding the goal of problem gambling treatment. One is whether the goal of treatment is to get the problem gambler to stop gambling or whether it is to identify and deal with those issues that led to gambling in the first place. The other is whether the goal of treatment is abstinence from gambling or controlled gambling in which less time and money are spent gambling, with a reduction in the harm that a person's gambling does to himself or herself and to others.

Strategies for treating problem gamblers fall into two broad categories: behavioral treatment, in which the emphasis is on changing the problem gambler's behavior, and cognitive treatment, which stresses changing the problem gambler's irrational thinking about many aspects of gambling. Relapse is a serious issue in problem gambling treatment. It is important that, when relapse occurs, problem gamblers not see it as failure and a reason to give up on treatment.

Very little of the small amount of research on the effectiveness of problem gambling treatment programs meets even relaxed standards of methodological rigor. No single treatment strategy seems better than any other. Combinations of behavioral and cognitive techniques, an emphasis on relapse reduction, and participation in Gamblers Anonymous can be effective in leading to abstinence from gambling, or at least a reduction in the harmful, uncontrolled gambling that is the hallmark of the problem gambler.

REFERENCES

Beck, A.T., Rush, A.J., Shaw, B.F., and Emery, G.: *Cognitive Therapy of Depression.* New York: Guilford, 1979.

Bergler, Edmund: *The Psychology of Gambling.* London: International Universities Press, [1957] 1970.

Blaszczynski, Alex, and Silove, Derrick: Cognitive and behavioral therapies for pathological gambling. *Journal of Gambling Studies,* *11*:195 220, 1995.

Custer, Robert, and Harry Milt: *When Luck Runs Out: Help for Compulsive Gamblers and Their Families.* New York: Facts on File Publications, 1985.

Dickerson, Mark: *Compulsive Gamblers.* London: Longman, 1984.

Dickerson, Mark, et. al.: Controlled gambling as a therapeutic technique for compulsive gamblers. *Journal of Behavior Therapy and Experimental Psychiatry, 10:*139-141, 1979.

Fingarette, Herbert: *Heavy Drinking: The Myth of Alcoholism as a Disease.* Berkeley: University of California Press, 1988.

Franklin, Joanna, and Thoms, Donald R.: Clinical observations of family members of compulsive gamblers. In Shaffer, Howard J., Stein, Sharon, Gambino, Blase, and Cummings, Thomas N. (Eds): *Compulsive Gambling: Theory, Research, and Practice,* Lexington, MA: Lexington Books, 135-146, 1989.

Hayano, David M.: *Poker Faces.* Berkeley: University of California Press, 1982.

Hollander, Eric, Frenkel, Maxim, DeCaria, Concetta, M., Trungold, Sari, and Stein, Dan J.: Treatment of pathological gambling with clomipramine. *American Journal of Psychiatry, 149*:710-711, 1992.

Hollander, Eric, DeCaria, Concetta M., Mario, Eduardo, Wong, Cheryl M., Mosovich, Serge, Grossman, Robert, and Begaz, Tomer: Short-term single-blind fluvoxamine treatment of pathological gambling. *American Journal of Psychiatry, 155*:1781-1783, 1989.

Lesieur, Henry R.: Costs and treatment of pathological gambling. *The Annals, 556*:153-169, 1998.

Lesieur, Henry R., and Blume, Sheila B.: Evaluation of patients treated for pathological gambling in a combined alcohol, substance abuse, and pathological gambling unit using the addiction severity index. *British Journal of Addiction, 86*:1017-1028, 1991.

Lorenz, Valerie C. and Yaffee, Robert A.: Pathological gamblers and their spouses: Problems in interaction. *Journal of Gambling Behavior, 5*:113-126, 1989.

McCown, William G., and Chamberlain, Linda L.: *Best Possible Odds: Contemporary Treatment Strategies for Gambling Disorders.* New York: Wiley, 2000.

Moskowitz, Joel A.: Lithium and lady luck: Use of lithium carbonate in compulsive gambling. *New York State Journal of Medicine, 80*: 785-788, 1980.

Oldman, David: Compulsive gamblers. *Sociological Review, 26*:349-370, 1978.

Pavalko, Ronald M.: *Risky Business: America's Fascination with Gambling.* Belmont, CA: Wadsworth, 2000.

Rankin, Howard: Control rather than abstinence as a goal in the treatment of excessive gambling. *Behavior Research and Therapy, 20*: 185 187, 1982.

Rosecrance, John: *Gambling Without Guilt.* Pacific Grove: Brooks/Cole, 1988.

Rosenthal, Richard J.: The psychodynamics of pathological gambling: A review of the literature. In Galski, Thomas (Ed.), *The Handbook of Pathological Gambling.* Springfield, IL, Charles C Thomas, 41-70, 1987.

Rugle, Loreen: The treatment of pathological gambling. Indianapolis, Indiana University Center for Urban Policy and the Environment, 1999.

Saiz, J.: No hagen juego, senores (Don't begin the game). *Interviu, 829*:24-28, 1992.

Schewan, D. and Brown, R.I.F.: The role of fixed interval conditioning in promoting involvement in off-course betting. In Eadington, William R. and Cornelius, Judy, *Gambling Behavior and Problem Gambling.* Reno, Institute for the Study of Gambling and Commercial Gaming, 111-132, 1993.

Scott, Marvin: *The Racing Game.* Chicago, Aldine, 1968.

Sharpe, L. and Tarrier, N.: Towards a cognitive-behavioral theory of problem gambling. *British Journal of Psychiatry, 162*:407-412, 1993.

Skinner, B.F.: *Science and Human Behavior.* New York: Free Press, 1953.

Stinchfield, Randy D., and Winters, Ken C.: Treatment effectiveness of six state-supported compulsive gambling treatment programs in Minnesota. Report to the Compulsive Gambling Treatment Program, Minnesota Department of Human Services, June, 1996.

Taber, Julian I., McCormick, Richard A., Russo, Angel M., Adkins, Bonnie J., and Ramirez, Luis F.: Follow-up of pathological gamblers after treatment. *American Journal of Psychiatry, 144*:757-761, 1987.

Walker, Michael B.: Treatment strategies for problem gambling: A review of effectiveness. In Eadington, William R. and Cornelius, Judy, *Gambling Behavior and Problem Gambling.* Reno, Institute for the Study of Gambling and Commercial Gaming, 533-566, 1993.

Wessler, R.L.: Cognitive psychotherapy approaches to personality disorders. *Piscologia Conductual, 1*: 45-48, 1993.

Chapter 8

GAMBLERS ANONYMOUS

The importance of Gamblers Anonymous (GA) in the treatment of problem gambling has been noted several times in previous chapters. This chapter provides a more thorough discussion of GA. In addition to identifying differences between GA and Alcoholics Anonymous (AA), this chapter also deals with the issue of how GA attempts to change people and just how successful it is in "treating" problem gamblers.

WHAT IS GAMBLERS ANONYMOUS?

GA is a "12 step" self-help recovery program. In many respects, it is modeled after the much better known AA recovery program, which started in 1935. One reason for this is that one of the founders of GA (known as "Jim W.") was also a recovering alcoholic and familiar with the AA program. In addition, AA has served (and continues to serve) as the model for self-help groups dealing with a wide range of "addictive" and problematic behaviors.

According to Gamblers Anonymous, the "Fellowship of Gamblers Anonymous" was founded in 1957 in Los Angeles by a recovering alcoholic and problem gambler known as "Jim W." He was joined in this effort by another gambler, "Sam J." However, a mild dispute exists over this starting date. According to other "unofficial" accounts, GA began in 1947 (Browne, 1994; Deland, 1950). What became of this initial effort is unclear, but the GA started in 1957 has been in operation continuously since that time. Two other groups are affiliated with GA. These are GamAnon, for family members and friends of problem gamblers, and GamaTeen, for the teenage children of problem gamblers.

GA is a private nonprofit organization that exists for the purpose of helping problem gamblers live lives free of gambling. The GA national organization and local GA chapters are self-supporting and do not accept outside contributions. It has more than 1,000 chapters worldwide. Some GA chapters are also informally affiliated with inpatient and outpatient treatment programs operated by VA hospitals, psychiatric hospitals, and a wide variety of addiction treatment and counseling programs. However, GA meetings are run by chapter members (i.e., problem gamblers), not by professional counselors.

DIFFERENCES BETWEEN GAMBLERS ANONYMOUS AND ALCOHOLICS ANONYMOUS

Despite similarities between the AA and GA recovery programs, there are some very important differences. Problem gamblers referred to AA meetings by well-meaning counselors unfamiliar with the nuances of problem gambling often respond by feeling that they "have nothing in common" with AA participants and may give up on treatment altogether. Twelve-step programs are not "one size fits all." AA should not be used for problem gamblers, unless they also have an alcohol problem, in which case participation in both programs is appropriate.

GA takes a different approach to spirituality than AA does. Compared with AA, there are fewer direct references to God, and when the word is used, it tends to get qualified in various ways. GA tends to be more pragmatic and secular, focusing on the cessation of gambling as the overriding goal of participation (Browne, 1994).

Although GA stresses the goal of achieving abstinence from gambling, it also acknowledges that gambling is a symptom of other problems. However, compared with AA, there is less concern with identifying and dealing with those problems, developing self-understanding, and less concern with character analysis and development. According to McCown and Chamberlain (2000), GA is more "tough minded," and there is less "hand holding" compared with AA. They note that the language used in GA can be "brutal and confrontational."

Another difference between GA and AA is "consciousness development." One of the AA "steps" refers to restoring members to "sanity." GA's comparable step stresses restoring members to a "normal" way of thinking and living. Browne (1991) has pointed out that GA has selectively adapted the AA program by stressing a "secular, medically oriented path" rather than AA's "spiritually oriented path."

According to several observers (Barlow, 1988; Baumeister et al., 1994; and McCown and Chamberlain, 2000), GA is more open to new treatment approaches and counseling strategies than AA is. Although both AA and GA have an "official" recovery literature and model, GA tends to be more willing to depart from that model and explore new options.

One feature of GA that does not seem to have an equivalent in AA is the "pressure relief" group meeting. After a period of abstinence from gambling, GA members can request a meeting that includes the gambler, the gambler's spouse or partner, and individual GA members (and often their partners and spouses) with longer periods of recovery. The focus of the meeting is on finances. This includes the development of a plan for repaying debts (both legal debts and loans from bookies and loan sharks) and the development of a household budget. Typically, the plan includes taking the gambler's name off of all financial accounts, turning control of money over to the spouse/partner, and putting the gambler on an allowance. In effect, the gambler's spouse/partner is urged to take control of and responsibility for household finances and the gambler's access to money. This is quite different from AA, in which the spouse/partner is urged to take less responsibility for the alcoholic.

Another difference has to do with how members perceive and redefine themselves. Participants in both GA and AA see themselves as different from other people. In effect, they label themselves as "deviants." However, there is a significant difference in how easily they can be "delabeled" (eliminate the deviant label) and be "relabeled" as nondeviant and develop an explanation for their behavior. The alcoholic's behavior is redefined as a physical illness over which one has no control. As pointed out earlier, the idea that alcoholism is a physical illness has become a widespread and culturally accepted way of understanding the behavior of alcoholics. In the case of problem gambling, there is no evidence of physical illness or disease, and the idea that the problem gambler is a "sick person" does not have anywhere near the same cultural acceptance. Consequently, it is more difficult for the problem gambler than the alcoholic to develop a new self-conception that has a culturally shared meaning (Preston and Smith, 1985).

In addition to the major differences between GA and AA just discussed, several "minor" differences are nevertheless important. One is that GA meetings tend to be longer than AA meetings, caused largely by the fact that GA meetings provide an opportunity for everyone to "give therapy" by talking about their and others' gambling problems. In addition, GA meetings tend to occur less frequently than AA meetings in most communities. GA's "pragmatic" orientation places less emphasis on systematically working through the "steps," which results in fewer step meetings (Browne, 1991, Lesieur, 1990).

The strength of GA lies in its reinforcement of the idea that the problem gambler's problems are shared and experienced by other people. That is what makes it a self-help *group*. How it accomplishes that involves what Browne (1991) has called a "selective adaptation" of the AA model.

Based on participant observation research in GA, Livingston (1974) describes the process of developing an attachment to and identification with GA as involving several stages. A crisis of some kind usually leads to initial attendance at a GA meeting. Although newcomers may experience anxiety about discussing their gambling problems in front of strangers, they are relieved to learn that "they are not alone." They find that others do not judge their behavior or ridicule them, because they have the same problem. Consequently, newcomers are able to be honest about their behavior and problems without being embarrassed. Gradually, they come to identify with other GA members, because their own experiences have been similar to those of others. Eventually, they internalize the GA conception of the nature of their problem and what they need to do to deal with it.

DOES GAMBLERS ANONYMOUS "WORK?"

Because GA does not keep records on the attendance and gambling activities of its members (i.e., it takes anonymity seriously), it is extremely difficult to evaluate how successful it is in helping its members achieve recovery. The same issues discussed in Chapter 7 regarding the evaluation of different kinds of treatment apply here, because GA can be regarded as a type of "treatment." What is success? Is it continued participation in GA? Is it abstinence? If so, for how long a period of time?

Only a few attempts have been made to evaluate the effectiveness of GA. The research that does exist suggests that GA is less effective than AA in achieving abstinence (Lesieur and Custer, 1984; Preston and Smith, 1975). One explanation for this is the issue discussed earlier regarding how alcoholism and problem gambling are defined and the ease with which alcoholics and problem gamblers can be "labeled" and "relabeled." The comparatively greater difficulty that exists in relabeling problem gamblers may account for at least some of the difference in the effectiveness of the two programs.

A study of first-time attenders of a GA meeting in Scotland illustrates the process by which some people continue to attend GA meetings and why others drop out. Both those who persist in attending and those who drop out indicated that they obtained useful information and advice and felt that they learned about their own problems by listening to others talk about their problems.

However, those who dropped out were more likely to believe that they could become "controlled gamblers." Compared with long-time members of GA and those newcomers who persisted in attending, the dropouts also believed that they had not yet reached a "low" as extreme as that of other members. This suggests that the gamblers with the most severe and intense problems continue attending and those who compare themselves with others and conclude that their problems are mild tend to drop out (Brown, 1986, 1987a, 1987b). Another British study of 232 GA participants found that only 8 percent were not gambling after one year, and that after two years 7 percent were totally abstinent from gambling (Stewart and Brown, 1988).

McCown and Chamberlain (2000) argue that "GA works as long as a person works GA." In other words, as long as a person is regularly attending meetings, the likelihood of gambling is reduced, and when relapses occur, they tend to be less frequent, less severe, and of shorter duration.

Although problem gambling counselors generally regard spousal involvement in treatment and in GamAnon as important, the impact of the spouse's involvement on the problem gambler's recovery is unclear. One small-scale study of the spouses of problem gamblers found that whether they participated or not in GamAnon was unrelated to the problem gambler's relapse (return to gambling) after beginning the recovery process (Zion et al., 1991). It is altogether possible, of course, that GamAnon participation can be beneficial for the spouse, even if it has no impact on the problem gambler's recovery.

SUMMARY

GA is a self-help group modeled in many ways after AA. However, there are significant differences between GA and AA. Compared to AA, GA places less emphasis on spirituality and focuses on stopping the problem gambler's gambling rather than exploring and dealing with the reasons for the gambling. GA also takes an eclectic, pragmatic approach to dealing with member's problems, following an "if it works, use it" approach.

GA stresses the importance of group support and shared experiences. The program attempts to redefine how problem gamblers perceive themselves and, in effect, tries to substitute "not gambling" for "gambling" as the central focus of the problem gambler's life.

Even fewer evaluations of the success of GA exist than there are of the treatment strategies used by individual counselors. Problem gambling counselors stress the importance of GA participation on the grounds that it reduces the likelihood of gambling and the frequency, severity, and duration of relapses.

REFERENCES

Barlow, D.H.: *Anxiety and its Disorders: The Nature of Treatment of Anxiety and Panic.* New York: Guilford Press, 1988.

Baumeister, R.F., Heatherton, T.F., and Tice, D.M.: *How and Why People Fail at Self-Regulation,* San Diego: Academic Press, 1994.

Brown, R.I.F.: Dropouts and continuers in Gamblers Anonymous: Life context and other factors. *Journal of Gambling Behavior, 2*:130-140, 1986.

Brown, R.I.F.: Dropouts and continuers in Gamblers Anonymous: Part 2. Analysis of free-style accounts of experiences with GA. *Journal of Gambling Behavior, 3*:68-79, 1987a.

Brown, R.I.F.: Dropouts and continuers in Gamblers Anonymous: Part 3. Some possible specific reasons for dropout. *Journal of Gambling Behavior, 3*:137-151, 1987b.

Browne, Basil R.: The selective adaptation of the Alcoholics Anonymous program by Gamblers Anonymous. *Journal of Gambling Studies, 7*:187-206, 1991.

Browne, Basil R.: Not really God: Secularization and pragmatism in Gamblers Anonymous. *Journal of Gambling Studies, 10*:247-260, 1994.

Deland, P.S.: The facilitation of gambling. *The Annals, 269*:21-29, 1950.

Lesieur, Henry R.: Working with and understanding Gamblers Anonymous. In Powell, T.J. (Ed.): *Working with Self Help*, Silver Spring, NASW Press, pp. 237-253, 1990.

Lesieur, Henry R., and Custer, Robert, L.: Pathological gambling: Roots, phases, and treatment. *The Annals, 474*:146-156, 1984.

Livingston, Jay: *Compulsive Gamblers: Observations on Action and Abstinence.* New York: Harper and Row, 1974.

McCown, William G., and Chamberlain, Linda L.: *Best Possible Odds: Contemporary Treatment Strategies for Gambling Disorders.* New York: Wiley, 2000.

Preston, Frederick W., and Smith, Ronald W.: Types and treatments of compulsive gambling: Transferring the AA Paradigm. Paper presented at the Second Annual Conference on Gambling, Lake Tahoe, June, 1975.

Preston, Frederick W., and Smith, Ronald W.: Delabeling and relabeling in Gamblers Anonymous: Problems with transferring the Alcoholics Anonymous paradigm. *Journal of Gambling Behavior, 1*:97-105, 1985.

Stewart, Ruth M., and Brown, R.I.F.: An outcome study of Gamblers Anonymous. *British Journal of Psychiatry, 152*:284-288, 1988.

Zion, Maxene M., Tracy, Elizabeth, and Abell, Neil: Examining the relationship between spousal involvement in Gam-Anon and relapse behaviors in pathological gamblers. *Journal of Gambling Studies, 7*:117-131, 1991.

Chapter 9

PUBLIC POLICY, TRAINING,
AND CERTIFICATION

Little attention has been devoted to problem gambling treatment by public policymakers. This chapter concludes with a discussion of what is occurring with regard to public and private sector initiatives to address the issue of problem gambling awareness, prevention, and treatment.

THE NATIONAL PICTURE

Currently, there is no national public policy regarding problem gambling. It is impossible to find a federal agency or program with a primary focus on any aspect of education about or research on problem gambling or its treatment. There is no problem gambling equivalent to, for example, the National Institute on Drug Abuse. The interest of the federal government in problem gambling has been limited to support for research on the prevalence of problem gambling and the sporadic funding of treatment for problem gamblers in some Veterans Administration hospitals. The issue of problem gambling also has not found its way on to the agendas of private foundations.

In 1976 the federal Commission on the Review of the National Policy toward Gambling did acknowledge the existence of problem gambling. Twenty years later, Congress passed and President Clinton signed the National Gambling Impact Study Commission Act of 1996. The nine-member Commission (NGISC) created by the Act was charged with studying the economic and social impacts of gambling in the United States, including the impact of problem gambling on individuals and their families. After numerous hearings and studies, the Commission complete its work and issued its report, including recommendations, in June 1999.

NGISC Recommendations

The NGISC made seventy-two major recommendations (several with subrecommendations), many of which bear directly or indirectly on the issue of problem gambling. All the recommendations discussed in the following are from the National Gambling Impact Study Commission Report (1999). The most important recommendation of the Commission was that the *states* are best equipped to regulate gambling within their borders, thus ensuring that there will not, in the foreseeable future, be a comprehensive, national policy on problem gambling or any other aspect of gambling. There are two exceptions to this recommendation. One is gambling on Native American reservations, because it is already regulated by federal statute, the Indian Gaming Regulation Act of 1988 (known as IGRA). The second exception is internet gambling. The rationale here is that, because the internet transcends state and even national borders, state regulation is impractical if not impossible.

Among the NGISC's recommendations, the following bear on the topic of problem gambling:

- That warnings regarding the risks and dangers of (problem) gambling should be posted in prominent locations in all gambling facilities
- That states should not authorize any more "convenience gambling" devices (such as lottery ticket sales machines, video lottery terminals, or slot machines) in "neighborhood outlets" (presumably shopping malls, convenience stores, bars, restaurants, etc.) and cease and roll back existing operations
- That state gambling regulatory agencies should ban "aggressive advertising," especially advertising that targets poor neighborhoods or youth

The Commission also recommended that state gambling regulatory agencies require all gambling facilities, as a condition of licensing, to adhere to the following practices:

- Adopt a clear policy on problem gambling
- Have a high-ranking executive responsible for overseeing the facility's policy on problem gambling
- Train management and staff to develop strategies for recognizing and dealing with customers whose gambling behavior suggests a gambling problem
- Refuse service to any customer whose gambling behavior exhibits indications of problem gambling and provide the customer with information on gambling treatment programs and self-help groups
- Provide insurance that makes treatment available for problem gambling among employees of gambling facilities

Another set of Commission recommendations urged states and Native American tribal governments to create a "Gambling Privilege Tax" that would essentially involve setting aside some of the profits from gambling activities (the amount was not specified) to be used for research, prevention, education, and treatment programs. Specific recommendations included:

- Undertaking research on the prevalence of problem gambling in the general population and among gambling facility patrons, with special attention given to problem gambling among youth, women, the elderly, and members of minority groups
- Identifing and maintaining a list of treatment providers and self-help groups
- Subsidizing the costs of treatment for problem gambling on the basis of financial need when private funding is not available

The Commission also recommended that states require private and public health insurers and managed care providers to identify successful treatment programs, educate participants in the programs about problem gambling, and cover appropriate treatment programs under their plans. If implemented, this would be a very significant advance, because, as indicated earlier, health insurance coverage for the treatment of problem gambling is virtually nonexistent.

Also recommended by the Commission were three policies long advocated by people involved in public awareness, prevention, and the treatment of problem gambling. One of these was having gambling facilities establish procedures for voluntary self-exclusion (i.e., having oneself "banned" from the facility). The second was requiring state run, approved, or licensed gambling facilities to conspicuously post and disseminate the telephone numbers of at least two providers of problem gambling information, referral, and treatment (e.g., the phone number of a state council's "helpline"). The final recommendation involves easy access to money. The Commission recommended that states and tribal governments ban credit card cash advance and other devices activated by debit or credit cards from the immediate gambling areas of gambling facilities.

Almost all of the recommendations presented to this point were directed at states and tribal governments. The Commission also made a number of recommendations to Congress. Most of them focus on authorizing or encouraging research by federal agencies to provide answers to the many unanswered questions that exist regarding problem gambling and its consequences.

For example, one recommendation was that the Substance Abuse and Mental Health Services Administration add a "gambling component" to its annual National Household Survey on Drug Abuse. In addition, the Commission recommended that federally funded longitudinal research consider adding a gambling component to its surveys, specifically questions that would provide information on gambling behavior, treatment-seeking, and the unmet need for treatment.

Another recommendation urged the National Institutes of Health to invite proposals for research on the effect of problem gambling on family members, divorce, spouse and child abuse, and suicide. Also recommended was research on the effect of problem gambling on workplace issues such as unemployment, loss of productivity, and workplace accidents, as well as research to measure the nonmonetary "social costs" of problem gambling, including divorce, domestic violence, child abuse and neglect, suicide, bankruptcy, and gambling-related crimes.

Because the federal Substance Abuse and Mental Health Services Administration conducts an annual survey of the providers of mental health services, the Commission recommended that this agency add questions to identify the availability of both private and public treatment services for problem gamblers and a description of the services they are receiving. Included in the recommendation is the collection of information on barriers to treatment, including lack of insurance coverage and a lack of qualified counselors.

As our review of treatment programs in Chapter 7 indicated, very little sound information exists on the success or "outcome" of different treatments. Relevant to this issue, the Commission recommended that an interdisciplinary research program be established to conduct outcome studies of treatment, including self-help groups such as Gamblers Anonymous.

Another set of recommendations was directed at the federal criminal justice system. The commission recommended that the National Institute of Justice engage in research to determine the impact of legal and illegal gambling on property and violent crime rates and add gambling components to ongoing studies of federal prison inmates, parolees, and probationers who have disorders that frequently coexist with problem gambling (e.g., depression, drug addiction).

Problem gambling among people employed in the gambling industry also received some attention from the Commission. Here the recommendation was that the National Institutes of Health stimulate research on the prevalence of problem gambling among the employees of casinos, racetracks, and lotteries (including people employed in selling lottery tickets in convenience stores, grocery stores, gas stations, etc.).

In November of 1993, the National Council on Problem Gambling (NCPG) issued a position paper calling for a national policy on problem gambling (National Council on Problem Gambling, 1993). The report was sent to all members of congress, federal cabinet officials, and the governors and attorneys general of all 50 states. The key recommendations in the NCPG's position paper included the inclusion of problem gambling and substance abuse in a national health care plan; a national survey to develop prevalence rates on problem gambling, a study of the social impacts and costs and benefits of legalized gambling, and an assessment of the impact of problem gambling on "at-risk" populations (youth, the elderly, women, minorities, and the medically indigent); the development of policies to address problem gambling in the federal criminal justice system and among military personnel, including problem gamblers under the same protections afforded those with other disabilities. It is apparent that most of the NCPG's concerns have been addressed in the NGISC's recommendations

Many of the Commission's recommendations reflect an important shift in how problem gambling is coming to be seen. They reflect a view of problem gambling as a "public health" issue, with problem gambling regarded as an issue analogous to mental health, alcoholism, and other drug addiction. This is consistent with the perspective developing among many researchers in the field of gambling studies (Korn and Shaffer, 1999).

The recommendations of the Commission constitute an ambitious agenda for dealing with problem gambling by governments and the gambling industry. Just how seriously they are taken by state and tribal governments and the U.S. Congress remains to be seen. In the first two years after the release of the NGISC's report, there was certainly no evidence of a legislative rush to implement these recommendations. A few agencies within the federal government have shown an increased interest in encouraging research on the causes and consequences of problem gambling. There has also been a noticeable increase in the display of brochures dealing with problem gambling and the helpline phone numbers of state councils in gambling facilities, especially casinos, but it is not clear whether this is a consequence of the Commission's recommendations or an independent trend.

THE TRAINING OF PROBLEM GAMBLING COUNSELORS

Leadership in the recognition of problem gambling as a treatable disorder and in promoting the need for well-trained counselors has come from the NCPG and its state affiliates. The NCPG and its affiliates are private nonprofit educational organizations that promote public education about problem gambling and the development of expertise in its treatment.

NCPG and its state affiliates also advocate public and gambling industry responsibility for the financing of education and research on problem gambling and the establishment of counselor training programs and treatment centers. The NCPG and its affiliates are *not* antigambling. They are not advocates for or against the further legalization of gambling.

NCPG can appropriately be regarded as a "social movement." It was founded in 1972 in New York. Its early members included recovering problem gamblers, recovering alcoholics, counselors, clergy, and a few academics in the fields of psychology and sociology. In recent years its membership has grown to include more psychiatrists, clinical psychologists, and an increasing number of academic and nonacademic psychologists, lawyers, economists, and sociologists, as well as members of the gambling industry. NCPG is not formally affiliated with Gamblers Anonymous, but many of its "recovering" members are also active in Gamblers Anonymous chapters. During its thirty-year history, the organization has not only grown in size but also broadened its membership base.

In 1985, NCPG began publishing the *Journal of Gambling Behavior*. In 1990 the journal's name was changed to the *Journal of Gambling Studies*, a change that coincided with its joint sponsorship by the NCPG and the Institute for the Study of Gambling and Commercial Gaming at the University of Nevada, Reno. Since 1987, the NCPG has held an annual "National Conference on Gambling Behavior" that draws participants from around the world. Both the journal and these annual conferences have contributed significantly to the establishment of "gambling studies" as a research specialty that goes well beyond just the understanding and treatment of problem gambling.

CERTIFICATION PROGRAMS

Certification is widespread throughout the health care industry. It is an acknowledgment that practitioners possess the expertise to do what they purport to do. As problem gambling treatment becomes part of the "public health" system, certification can be expected to become increasingly important.

There are three national certification programs. In addition to the NCPG's "National Gambling Counselor Certification," the American Academy of Health Care Providers in Addictive Disorders, based in Massachusetts, offers certification as a "Certified Gambling Specialist," and certification is also available through the American Compulsive Gambling Counselor Certification Board, which is operated by the Council on Compulsive Gambling of New Jersey. Table 9.1 presents information describing these programs.

The requirements of these certification programs vary somewhat. However, they all emphasize a strong core of gambling-specific training and experience counseling problem gamblers.

TABLE 9.1
NATIONAL GAMBLING COUNSELOR CERTIFICATION PROGRAMS

	American Compulsive Gambling Counselor Certification Board	National Gambling Counselor Certification	American Academy of Health Care Providers in the Addictive Disorders Certified Gambling Specialist
Sponsoring Agency	Council on Compulsive Gambling of New Jersey	National Council on Problem Gambling	American Academy of Health Care Providers in the Addictive Disorders
Educational Requirements	None	Minimum of high school diploma or equivalency	No specific criteria, but supervision requirements differ for those with MA degree and those with less than MA or no degree
Training hours	142 clock hrs covering core problem gambling curriculum within a 5 year period	Minimum of approved gamling specific training hours; documentation of additional 300 hours of related training or education (e.g., chemical dependency, psychology, social work, etc.)	Minimum of 60 hours of gambling specific training
Supervision hours	180 practical training hours under qualified supervision in a recognized treatment facility	At least two one hour sessions per month for a minimum of 12 months (24 hours)	None specified
Direct contact hours	750 hours within a 3 year period	2000 hours (or one year full time equivalent to problem/pathological gamblers and significant others in a Board approved supervisor	MA level: 3 full years direct experience with addictive disorders, a meaningful portion of caseload must be with problem/pathological gamblers. Less than MA degree or no degree: 5 years supervised clinical experience

Other Requirements	No active addiction (gambling, alcohol, or drugs) in 2 years prior to application; attendance at at least 15 GA meetings	None	Written examination
Fees	$200	$175	$205
Recertification	Every 2 years	Every 3 years	

Source: Rugle, Loreen: The treatment of pathological gambling. Indianapolis, Indiana University Center for Urban Policy and the Environment, 1999, p.32. Reprinted by permission.

In addition to these national programs, many of the state councils on problem gambling and the Canadian Foundation on Compulsive Gambling also provide appropriate gambling-specific training for counselors, providing an important entry point into the field of problem gambling counseling.

THE STATE LEVEL

Only a few states have moved to certify or license problem gambling counselors. The few that have (Mississippi, Michigan, and Ohio) have established certification requirements similar to the requirements of the three national certification programs. For example, Mississippi has established two levels of certification. Certified Compulsive Gambling Counselor I (CCGC I) and Certified Compulsive Gambling Counselor II (CCGC II). CCGC I certification requires (1) 30 hours of gambling specific training, (2) 2000 supervised direct contact hours (including 250 hours with problem gamblers and their families and 250 hours with people with other addictions), and (3) either certification as an addictions counselor, licensure as a mental health professional, or completion of a master's degree in a mental health field. CCGC II certification requires (1) 60 hours of gambling-specific training, (2) 2000 supervised direct contact hours with problem gamblers and their families, and (3) certification or licensure as a mental health professional and at least a bachelor's degree in counseling or a related mental health field (Rugle, 1999).

A good deal of effort at the state level has been aimed at getting legislatures, state gaming commissions, and state departments of human services to provide funding for public education, toll-free telephone "helplines," counselor training, and treatment programs.

At the state level, support for public education, prevention, and the treatment of problem gambling has been modest at best. In 1996, only 21 states were operating or had provided funding for programs dealing with some aspect of problem gambling. It has been estimated that in 1996 states had allocated $13 million for education, research, and treatment. Although that figure may seem large in an absolute sense, it is small by comparison with funding for other human service programs. For example, although Texas provided $2 million per year (mainly from lottery profits) for problem gambling, in fiscal year 1997 the state-funded alcohol and drug abuse programs provided $122 million (Cox et al, 1997). Clearly, a relatively low priority is given to problem gambling by state policies.

However, some evidence exists that states and gambling enterprises are beginning to do more. Information on funding for problem gambling issues from public and gambling industry sources in 1998 is presented in Table 9.2.

TABLE 9.2
1998 ALLOCATIONS FOR PROBLEM GAMBLING PROGRAMS, BY STATE

State	Sources	Allocation
Alabama	None	None
Arkansas	None	None
Arizona	9 Indian casinos, 2 racetracks, 1 non-Indian casino management company	$ 170,000
California	Indian casinos, racetracks, card clubs	89,000
Colorado	Lottery	25,000
Connecticut	2 Indian casinos, 1 non-Indian casino management company, lottery, racetracks, other	1,190,000
Delaware	State general revenues	1,025,000
Florida	Lottery, 1 non-Indian casino management company, 4 racetracks	
Georgia	Lottery	200,000
Hawaii	None	None
Idaho	None	None
Illinois	Casino Gaming Association (riverboats)	500,000
Indiana	Riverboat admission tax, 1 racetrack, other	813,000
Iowa	State (% of revenues from lottery, riverboat casinos, and slots at racetracks)	3,015,000

Kansas	None	None
Kentucky	Lottery, other	104,000
Louisiana	Riverboat Gaming Association, 6 non-Indian casinos, Lottery, other	775,000
Maine	None	None
Maryland	None	None
Massachusetts	State Department of Public Health	1,100,000
Michigan	Lottery, casinos, other	133,000
Minnesota	Lottery, Indian casinos, non-Indian casino management companies, general revenues	2,030,250
Mississippi	Mississippi Gaming Association (riverboats), casinos, general revenues	290,000
Missouri	Missouri Riverboat Gaming Association, Lottery, other	1,020,000
Nebraska	Lottery	185,000
Nevada	General revenues, 1 casino operator, donations	345,000
New Hampshire	None	None
New Jersey	Casinos, racetracks, general revenues	720,000
New Mexico	Responsible Gaming Committee	36,000
New York	State office of Mental Health	1,564,000
North Carolina	None	None
North Dakota	General revenues	50,000
Ohio	Lottery	350,000
Oklahoma	None	None
Oregon	Lottery	2,600,000
Pennsylvania	Lottery, racetracks	72,000
Rhode Island	Lottery, general revenues	15,000
South Carolina	Casino operator	50,000
South Dakota	Unknown	200,000
Tennessee	None	None
Texas	Texas Commission on Alcohol and Drug Abuse	475,000
Utah	None	None
Vermont	None	None
Virginia	Lottery	36,000
Washington	State Gaming Commission, Lottery, other	159,000
West Virginia	None	None
Wisconsin	Lottery, 1 Indian casino	135,000
Wyoming	None	None

Source: National Council on Problem Gambling: *1998 Allocations for Problem Gambling Programs by State,* www.naspl.org/pgambcht.html, downloaded March 9, 2000. Reprinted by permission.

By 1998, 33 states had funding available for problem gambling programs dealing with education, prevention, and treatment, and almost $19.5 million was available for such programs. It is difficult to discern very many consistent patterns in this funding. It is noteworthy that

Nevada, New Jersey, and Mississippi, the three states with the largest casino industries, are relatively low (although not the lowest) in terms of funding for any aspect of problem gambling. Oregon, Iowa, and Minnesota, which have Native American reservation casinos, riverboat casinos, lotteries, and racing (in varying combinations), have the highest levels of funding.

Although funding for problem gambling education, awareness, prevention, and treatment seems to be improving over time, difficulties remain. Funding from public sources typically has to be legislated on an annual or biennial basis, and the reduction or withdrawal of funding is commonplace. This unpredictability of funding makes planning and continuity of programs difficult. It also suggests that public policymakers give the issue of problem gambling a relatively low priority.

GAMBLING INDUSTRY INITIATIVES

The gambling industry itself (especially the casino segment) has also played an important role in making problem gambling a serious public policy issue. For example, since the late 1980s, the Promus Corporation, which operates Harrah's Hotels and Casinos in Nevada and Atlantic City, as well as several riverboat casinos, has had a compulsive gambling education, intervention, and counseling program for its employees. It also led the way with casino signage calling attention to problem gambling by promoting the idea of "responsible gaming." Its signage includes catchy slogans like "Gamble with your head, not over it" and "Know when to stop before you get started" (the latter on a traffic stop sign). It recently has been exploring ways of intervening with customers exhibiting signs of problem gambling and promoting the idea of "responsible gaming" within the gambling industry as a whole.

Perhaps the most significant initiative has come from within the gambling industry. The American Gaming Association (AGA) is the gambling industry's national trade and lobbying association. In 1996, the AGA created the "National Center for Responsible Gaming." Located in Kansas City, Missouri, the Center's task is "to promote research and collect information on problem and underage gambling . . . and to . . . fund research; create prevention, intervention and treatment strategies; act as a national clearinghouse for research findings; and provide assistance to state and local governments to encourage responsible gaming practices" (American Gaming Association, 1997).

These gambling industry efforts are important for a number of reasons. They represent an acknowledgment of the existence of problem gambling (industry spokespersons and the American Gaming Association prefer the terms "problem gaming" and "problem gamer"). Substantial funding for these efforts has come from major casino gambling corporations, and these industry initiatives have attracted the attention of public officials who, with a few important exceptions, have not given the issue of problem gambling the attention it needs. In effect, the gambling industry has filled a vacuum created by the absence of a meaningful national policy on problem gambling.

Another indicator of concern with problem gambling within the industry is the attention the topic gets at gambling industry trade shows and conventions. The annual "World Gaming Congress & Expo," held in Las Vegas, has given increasing attention to problem gambling over the past decade. Recent meetings have included sessions on problem gambling conducted by nationally recognized experts on the topic and targeted at management in various sectors of the gambling industry, not just the casino segment. It seems that the gambling industry is becoming increasingly concerned about an aspect of the business that could be a potential source of criticism if not hostility toward it. In effect, it is in the gambling industry's self-interest to support efforts to prevent and treat problem gambling (Connor, 1996).

Despite these developments within the gambling industry, there are some indications that concern about problem gambling may not be all that widely shared throughout the industry. Articles in *International Gaming and Wagering Business* magazine (the industry's primary trade publication) frequently criticize casinos for not giving more attention to the issue of problem gambling (e.g. Palermo, 1998).

Some of the marketing practices of casinos are also at odds with this professed commitment to the promotion of "responsible gaming." Most casinos target frequent, heavy gamblers for special promotions and complimentary gifts (known as "comps"), including such things as free travel, rooms, meals, show tickets, and the like). Casinos will, for example, offer free rooms and meals to heavy gamblers whether they are losing or winning. Keeping the losers around longer increases the likelihood that they will "chase their losses" and lose even more. Keeping winners around is also in the self-interest of casinos; having won, they are likely to continue playing and eventually give their winnings back as the casino's advantage built into the games and the laws of probability have time to catch up with them.

A few casinos have also developed credit cards that people can use to accumulate points and bonuses redeemable at casino properties. They are similar to credit cards tied to airline"frequent flyer" programs, in which a dollar charged earns a mile. Ironically, Harrah's, the most prominent leader in the "responsible gaming" movement, has a card issued through VISA that accumulates points that can be redeemed at Harrah's casinos. Caesars also issues what could be characterized as a "frequent gambler's" credit card that earns bonus checks redeemable for chips at cashier cages in Caesars casinos (Gwynne, 1997; Horovitz, 1997). Finally, the easy availability of machines that will dispense instant cash through credit cards in casinos (a feature of gambling venues strongly criticized by the National Gambling Impact Study Commission) and the liberal use of "markers" (short-term, no interest loans to gamblers by casinos) seem inconsistent with the industry's verbal commitment to the promotion of "responsible gaming".

SUMMARY

Although alcohol and other drug addiction have been a national priority for some time, there has not been a national policy regarding problem gambling. The recommendations of the National Gambling Impact Study Commission represent the beginnings of such a policy, emphasizing prevention, education, and the development of treatment resources. Whether these recommendations get translated into action by state governments, Native American tribes operating casinos, and the private, commercial gambling industry remains to be seen.

The training of problem gambling counselors occurs at both the national and state levels. At the state level, it is being promoted by nonprofit "state councils on problem gambling." Nationally, three organizations offer training and certification. These are the National

Council on Problem Gambling, the American Academy of Health Care Providers in Addictive Disorders, and the American Compulsive Gambling Counselor Certification Board.

In recent years state governments operating lotteries and licensing and taxing gambling businesses (casinos, racetracks) have slowly increased funding (usually from lottery profits) for problem gambling education, awareness, prevention, and treatment. The private gambling industry, through the American Gaming Association, has also made important efforts to promote a commitment to "responsible gaming," especially within the casino segment of the gambling industry.

REFERENCES

American Gaming Association: News Release, January 28, 1997.

Connor, Matt: Gaming's ball and chain: Problem gambling, more than any other issue, curbs the growth of the casino, lottery, and parimutuel industries. *International Gaming and Wagering Business, 17*:1, 64-66, 68, 71, October, 1996.

Cox, Sue, Lesieur, Henry R., Rosenthal, Richard J., and Volberg, Rachel A.: Problem and Pathological Gambling in America: The National Picture. Columbia, MD, National Council on Problem Gambling, 1997.

Gwynne, S.C.: How casinos hook you. *Time*, 68-69, November 27, 1997.

Horovitz, Bruce: Harrah's rolls out VISA card with reward plan. *USA Today*, October 23, 1997.

Korn, David A., and Shaffer, Howard J.: Gambling and the health of the public: Adopting a public health perspective. *Journal of Gambling Studies, 15*:289-365, 1999.

National Council on Problem Gambling: The Need for a National Policy on Problem and Pathological Gambling in America. New York: National Council on Problem Gambling, November 1, 1993.

National Gambling Impact Study Commission Report, Washington, DC, www.ngisc.gov, downloaded June 18, 1999.

Palermo, Dave: Admitting there's a problem. *International Gaming and Wagering Business, 19*:40, January, 1998.

Rugle, Loreen: The treatment of pathological gambling. Indianapolis, Indiana University Center for Urban Policy and the Environment, 1999.

AUTHOR INDEX

SUBJECT INDEX